Olivier Messiaen

Twayne's Music Series

Chris Frigon and Camille Roman,
Consulting Editors

Olivier Messiaen

Carla Huston Bell

Twayne Publishers

Olivier Messiaen

Carla Huston Bell

Published in 1984
by Twayne Publishers
A Division of G. K. Hall & Company
70 Lincoln Street, Boston, Massachusetts 02111

Printed on permanent/durable
acid-free paper and bound in
the United States of America.

First Printing

This book was designed
by Barbara Anderson and typset
in Century Oldstyle by Compset, Inc.

0-8057-9457-3

10 9 8 7 6 5 4 3 2 1
First Printing

Contents

Olivier Messiaen
Courtesy of Herbert H. Breslin, Inc.

About the Author

Carla Huston Bell was born in Glendive, Montana, on May 11, 1944, and became involved with music at an early age. A pianist and violinist, she attended Montana State University on a violin scholarship where she received a Bachelor of Arts degree with honors. After winning several major musical competitions as a performing artist, she came to New York where she continued her studies, which included training in organ, voice, and theatre arts.

Her professional career began in television where she has performed on all major networks. Carla has played leading and supporting roles on Broadway and Off-Broadway; she has appeared with the New York City Opera Company and in repertory with the American Shakespeare Festival in Stratford, Connecticut. Her work in music and theatre has covered the east and west coasts as well as major cities in the United States.

After the birth of her two sons, Carla won an assistantship at Columbia University where she earned a Master of Arts Degree in 1973. In 1975 she received a Masters of Education Degree; her focus during these years was theory and composition rather than performance. Carla developed her talents in composition and has many published works and awards to her credit. She has been an ASCAP member for ten years.

Her studies centered on Olivier Messiaen with the pursuit of her doctorate degree, which she received in 1977 from Columbia University. Carla has taught music theory and composition in the Dalton School, New York City, and is presently the Director of Music at Trinity School, New York City. She has published articles in scholarly journals and has served as music critic for *Music Journal* in New York. A member of the International League of Women Composers, she was Faculty Coordinator for their conference on twentieth century music by women composers in 1980. Some of her works are listed in the recent publication, *Women in American Music*.

Preface

Olivier Messiaen is one of the most important figures in twentieth-century music, not only as an innovator in the field of composition, but as an educator who has exerted much influence over his young avant-garde students.

Born on December 10, 1908, in Avignon, Messiaen claims in his heart to be a Dauphinois, having stated that he loves passionately all mountains in general, and in particular, those of the Dauphine. His Flemish roots go back more than two centuries. It has been said that Flemish art is characterized by mystery and fantasy, and Olivier Messiaen frequently reveals a connection to his origins by the statement that he has within him the love of all things mysterious and marvelous.

Who is Olivier Messiaen? This question has been asked by many people and there have been many opinions advanced on the subject. Messiaen himself has patiently answered questions and has even written a great deal of personal information in his prefaces, notes to works, and so on. Despite the interviews, articles, and notes, however, there still remains a mystery about the man, and an air of incredulity concerning the religious nature that is at his center. Furthermore, there is need for an understanding of the special combination of musical and compositional techniques that Messiaen has used in the creation of his work throughout his career.

Messiaen has devoted more than sixty of his seventy-plus years to the world of music. Although he was born into a highly cultured and literary family, his interest in music was not directed by either of his parents. His father was a professor of English who made well-known translations of works of Shakespeare. His mother was the poetess, Cécile Sauvage. During her pregnancy with Messiaen she wrote a book of poetry called *L'ame en bourgeon* ("The Flowering Soul") in which she addressed the child that she was carrying. Messiaen believes his destiny was influenced by this spiritual bond with his mother.

Messiaen began his exploration of the piano on his own at the age of eight. He was self-taught until the family moved to Nantes, where he met his first teacher, Jehan de Gibon. During this early period Messiaen had already begun to compose music, which suggests that, as is the case with great composers, the vocation had already chosen the artist. Messiaen became conscious of this vocational choice when, at the age of ten, his teacher presented him with the score of Debussy's *Pelléas and Mélisande.* It was so inspiring to the young musician that his awareness of his own destiny was immediate and incontrovertible.

Messiaen's own first composition, entitled *La Dame de Shalotte,* for piano, was written in 1917. His first published work was the organ piece *Le banquet céleste* (1928). Messiaen has steadily followed his vocation as composer, and in doing so has written music that has consistently provided new innovations in contemporary music. From the time of his invention of original "modes of limited transposition" five decades ago to the present, Messiaen has sought his own means of expression, pushing beyond the boundaries of what had previously existed.

The musical excellence of this composer also extends to the areas of performance and education. He is a brilliant organist and for more than forty-seven years has been the organist of the Church of la Sainte Trinité in Paris. Messiaen has also been a professor of music at the renowned Paris Conservatory for more than thirty-five years, where his influence on the contemporary scene has been virtually immeasurable. At this point one might ask, What does Messiaen's music bring to the crucial changes that have emerged in the twentieth century? What influence has Messiaen had in directing the course of music during the critical midcentury period? What makes his music important in the evolution of music history?

Although his work as a composer is not yet finished, Messiaen has already provided a valuable legacy in the field of composition. He has written some of the most exquisitely beautiful works of this century and has earned a growing worldwide audience. *Vingt regards sur l'Enfant Jésus* ("Twenty Gazes upon the Infant Jesus") for piano is a work of two and a half hours that demands complete dedication on the part of the performing artist, as well as a formidable technique. *Quatuor pour la fin du temps* ("Quartet for the End of Time"), written while Messiaen was a prisoner of war in Tunis, is scored for violin, cello, clarinet, and piano. Messiaen has written several song cycles, two of which, *Poèmes pour Mi* and *Chants de terre et de ciel,* appear regularly in the concert repertoire of leading soprano artists.

The Tristan trilogy, one of his most important works, includes the *Turangalîla-symphonie,* which has received several performances in the United States. *Les offrandes oubliées* is another orchestral work that is regularly scheduled in the seasonal repertoire of American symphony orchestras. During recent years, several of Messiaen's orchestral works have been performed by the New York Philharmonic and other major orchestras throughout this country. The world premiere of *Des canyon aux étoiles* ("From the Canyon to the Stars") and *Et exspecto resurrectionem mortuorum* ("And I Await the Resurrection of the Dead") received an overwhelmingly enthusiastic reception in New York City.

These and numerous other works by this composer are stylistically so original that they are often immediately recognizable to the listener as the work of Messiaen. His highly individual style was arrived at through sincere dedication to every one of its elements. A cursory examination of these elements does not provide the key to understanding his technique and theoretical practice because of the breadth of study involved. This is probably the main reason that his music has not yet been examined or discussed in the detail it deserves. In reading about Messiaen one learns that among the influences on his work are the Catholic Church, plainchant, Greek and Indian rhythms, Stravinsky, birdsong, and the Tristan myth. The Messiaen devotee is thus provided with vast areas to examine. With thorough understanding of the specific nature of each of these influences and the way they blend into the total sound that is Messiaen's own, the music itself becomes more accessible to the listener.

Messiaen's importance on the contemporary music scene extends even further than the legacy of compositions that should ensure a hearing in future centuries. His presence in the midst of the avant-garde during the last three or four decades has been of crucial importance to the direction of modern music.

The illumination of how Messiaen's music has contributed to a creative epoch of infinite possibility is made possible by further knowledge of his musical language and techniques. Further examination throughout this book of his use of modes, his rhythmic invention, his interest in birdsong and Greek rhythms will increase the reader's awareness of just how he was able to further twentieth-century music. In addition to the concept of "total organization" that was introduced by Messiaen, it is likely that he has been responsible for the most significant development in rhythmic practice in the last three hundred years.

It is perhaps sufficient to point out that Messiaen is already firmly established in the hierarchy of the world's living composers. Like all great composers, his music is stimulating and inspiring, and it is my belief that it will be a very long time before it is forgotten. His music appears to be growing in its appeal to many types of listeners of all ages. Once listeners discover Messiaen, they tend to find his personal musical language and his originality of thought highly appealing. All the facets of the man and the composer seem to be interwoven, necessitating an understanding of both in order to comprehend the whole.

Why does the music of certain great composers appeal to people before they understand its complexities? Possibly it is due to the directness, the emotional language that speaks from the heart of the composer to the listener. Surely this may be one of the tests of a composer's power and may even be the final true test that separates greatness from mediocrity.

This book undertakes two tasks: to provide a structural and stylistic analysis of representative works by Olivier Messiaen, and to illuminate his contribution to the evolution of music of the twentieth century. The works selected for analysis meet the following requirements: (1) they cover the four performance media of organ, piano, instrumental ensemble, and voice; (2) they cover a wide area of Messiaen's lengthy creative life; and (3) they are representative of characteristics of Messiaen's style and compositional techniques.

I have chosen movements from various larger works rather than confine the study to one or two complete works, because in this way I was better able to satisfy the criteria I believe to be important. This choice was also determined by the conviction that full analysis is more helpful to the reader, and that it is therefore preferable to discuss whole movements rather than fragments.

The analysis examines compositional techniques of Messiaen from the perspectives of form, harmony, timbre, melody, and rhythm. Knowledge of the craftsmanship involved often assists in the appreciation of a work. This is especially true of a musician like Messiaen whose practices are not typical of other well-known composers. With knowledge of the process involved in his shorter works or complete movements, the reader has the tools to apply in analyzing the larger and more complex orchestral works.

I hope that this book will contribute to a better understanding of Messiaen's music, and to the understanding of contemporary idioms in general. I would like to acknowledge my gratitude to the various music instructors who, throughout my career, have worked with me as a performing artist, musician, composer, and theorist. I am forever indebted to my father, and to my mother Idamae, who began my musical training and who encouraged all facets of my musical growth.

My thanks go to the following publishers for permission to reproduce excerpts from Messiaen's music: Alphonse Leduc & Cie., Paris, France; Theodore Presser Co., representative for Durance & Cie., Paris, France; and Editions Salabert, Paris, France. In addition I am grateful to the publisher of *Music Journal* who allowed the use of material from the article "Olivier Messiaen" by Carla Huston Bell.

Special thanks are due to Twayne Series editor, Mr. John LaBine for his assistance, encouragement, editing, and fine insight during the preparation of this book.

Finally, I express my indebtedness to my family, particularly my sons Forrest and Rhahime, whose understanding, patience and adaptability contributed to the completion of the work.

Carla Huston Bell

Trinity School

Chronology

1908 Olivier Eugene Charles Prosper Messiaen is born in Avignon, France, December 10.

1916 Attends Lycee in Grenoble; composes first piece, *La Dame de Shallot.*

1918 Receives first music lessons in Nantes.

1919 Enters Paris Conservatory to study music.

1925 Wins first prize for counterpoint and fugue at Paris Conservatory.

1927 Wins first prize for piano accompaniment at Paris Conservatory.

1929 Wins first prize for organ, improvisation, and history of music.

1930 Wins first prize for composition. Publishes *Préludes pour piano.*

1931 Becomes organist of the Church of la Sainte Trinité, Paris.

1934 Begins appointment to teach chamber music and piano sight-reading at the Ecole Normale de Musique.

1935 Composes *La nativité du Seigneur* for organ, and premieres work at La Trinité.

1936 Marries violinist Claire Delbos. Receives appointment to teach organ improvisation at the Schola Cantorum. Founds *La Jeune France.*

1937 Son Pascal is born in Boulogne-Billancourt, France. Serves as music critic for *Revue Musicale.*

1939 France and Great Britain declare war on Germany; Messiaen enlists in army.

1940 Becomes prisoner of war and is taken to Germany; France surrenders to Germany.

1941   Composes *Quatuor pour la fin du temps* in Stalag 8A in Silesia and performs work before prison audience; subsequently is freed from prison to return to France.

1942   Receives appointment as Professor of Harmony at Paris Conservatory.

1943   Begins composition classes at the home of Guy Bernard-Delapierre.

1944   Writes *Technique de mon langage musical.*

1945   First performance of *Vingt regards sur l'Enfant Jésus,* with pianist Yvonne Loriod. Premieres *Trois petite liturgies de la presence divine,* which caused a great controversy among the critics.

1947   Founds class in analysis at Paris Conservatory. Teaches course in musical analysis at the Budapest Conservatory.

1949   Gives course in composition at the Berkshire Music Center at Tanglewood. Presents premiere United States performance of *Turangalîla-symphonie,* commissioned by Serge Koussevitzky and the Koussevitzky Foundation for the Boston Symphony. Conductor, Leonard Bernstein. Composes the first totally organized work, *Mode de valeurs et d'intensitiés.*

1950   Premieres *Cinq rechants* (1949) for mixed choir of twelve voices a capella.

1951   Gives premiere performance of *Messe de la Pentecôte* (1950) at Pentecost service, la Trinité.

1953   Presents first performance of *Le livre d'orgue* at Stuttgart.

1955   Gives Paris premiere of *Le livre d'orgue* at Church of la Sainte Trinité.

1959   Presents Yvonne Loriod at the concerts of Domaine Musical in premiere of *Catalogue d'oiseaux* for piano. First wife, Claire, dies after a long illness.

1960   Premieres *Chronochromie* at the Donaueschingen Festival.

1962   Marries pianist Yvonne Loriod. Visits Japan with Yvonne Loriod. Seiji Ozawa conducts *Turangalîla-symphonie* in Tokyo.

1963 Premieres *Sept haïkaï*, Japanese sketches, conducted by Pierre Boulez at the Domaine Musical.

1964 Visits the Argentine and gives course in rhythm at Buenos Aires. Premieres *Couleurs de la cité céleste* at Donaueschingen Festival, conducted by Pierre Boulez.

1966 Receives appointment to Professor of Composition at the Paris Conservatory. Premieres *Et exspecto resurrectionem mortuorum* at the Domaine Musical under Pierre Boulez.

1967 Becomes guest of honor at Olivier Messiaen Festival in Paris, Palais de Chaillot. Wins election by unanimous vote to the Institut de France, Academie des Beaux Arts. Gives First Concours de piano "Olivier Messiaen" for contemporary music at Royan (First Prize winner: Michel Beroff).

1968 Attends Messiaen Week at Dusseldorf for his sixtieth birthday.

1970 Tours United States and Canada.

1971 Receives Erasmus Prize at Amsterdam given by Queen Juliana and Prince Bernhard.

1972 Gives first performance of the *Meditations sur le mystère de la Sainte Trinité* for organ by the composer at the National Shrine of the Immaculate Conception in Washington. Receives Sibelius Prize in Helsinki; awarded Doctor honoris causi by Catholic University of the United States. Gives first performance in the United States of *La transfiguration de notre Seigneur Jésus-Christ,* conducted by Antal Dorati, Washington National Orchestra, Princeton Choir, Yvonne Loriod, at the Kennedy Center. *La transfiguration* at New York, Carnegie Hall. Presents first performance of *La fauvette des jardins* by Yvonne Loriod at the Espace Pierre Cardin in Paris.

1973 Receives honors at various festivals, including Messiaen Week in Dusseldorf, Cardiff, London, Flanders and United States. Elected Doctor of Literature at Cornell College, Iowa. Receives nomination as Member of the Academy of Arts and Sciences, Boston, Massachusetts.

1974 Attends Messiaen Week at Karlsruhe for his sixty-fifth birthday.

1975 Celebrates premiere of *Des canyons aux étoiles,* commissioned by Musica Aeterna, at Alice Tully Hall, New York City, Frederick Waldman conductor.

1976 Receives overwhelmingly enthusiastic reception of *Et exspecto resurrectionem mortuorum* at Avery Fisher Hall, New York City, Pierre Boulez conducting the New York Philharmonic Orchestra.

1978–1979 Tours the major cities of United States, culminating in Messiaen Week at New York's Lincoln Center in honor of his seventieth birthday.

1

Major Influences

The Family

Olivier Messiaen has a highly artistic personality; he has been totally committed throughout his life to the expression of his creative powers, devoted to nature and, above all, to the Roman Catholic faith. It would be impossible to comprehend his music without some understanding of his background and influences. The music reflects the integrity of expression and diverse interests of a man who has pursued those facets in art that have the most meaning to him. By examining the influences of family, teachers, preexisting musical materials, and admired composers, one begins to see the logic, coherence, and structure in his style.

Olivier Eugene Charles Prosper Messiaen was born in Avignon, France, on December 10, 1908, half-Flemish, half-Provençal. His mother, the celebrated poetess, Cécile Sauvage, was his strongest early influence. While pregnant with Olivier, she wrote a book of poetry which she dedicated to her yet unborn son. Throughout the book, entitled *L'ame en bourgeon* ("The Flowering Soul"), she wrote of her child with premonitions of his future greatness:

. . . je porte en moi l'amour
des choses mysteriuses et marveillouses.

(". . . I carry within me the love of
mysterious and marvelous things.")

Great composers often are born of ancestors who were gifted artistically and intellectually. Olivier Messiaen is not an exception. His father,

1

Pierre was a professor of English who produced a well-known translation of Shakespeare. When Messiaen was six, Pierre was transferred to Grenoble. Just as the family arrived in the city, however, World War I broke out, and the father was called to serve. Cécile Sauvage moved her two sons (Alain was four years younger than Olivier) to her brother's apartment in Grenoble, where they lived for the duration of the war.

During these childhood years Messiaen began to show a strong fascination with mysterious, magical, and supernatural things. His world from day to day became an atmosphere of Shakespearean heroes. Shakespeare meant all the human passions as well as the magic of elves, fairies, weird phantoms, and apparitions. Among the characters he much admired were King Lear, Puck, and Ariel; but his favorite play was *Macbeth,* particularly because of the witches and Banquo's ghost. He built sets for the plays out of brightly colored cellophane and became the star of all his performances, acting before a spellbound audience of one, his younger brother Alain.

This world of make-believe was enhanced by the spiritual and creative qualities of Messiaen's mother. Cécile Sauvage immersed her sons in the Catholic faith; this factor also influenced his early childhood imagination and later became a vital element in his musical creativity.

Although Olivier Messiaen came from a family of writers, poets, and cultivated ancestors who loved music, he was the first to express his generous creative talents in music. At eight he went to the Lyceé in Grenoble. On returning home, he sat at the piano and worked out by ear the music of Mozart's *Don Giovanni* and Berlioz's *Damnation of Faust.* The ability to teach himself to play the piano came as a great surprise to his family. He continued to demonstrate signs of significant musical talent; his ear showed tremendous sensitivity and his imaginative adventures in hearing harmonic vibrations presupposed his exceptional gifts. In the first decade of his life, he thus proved that he was a prodigy, not only through the reading and performing of Shakespeare at the age of eight, but in musical areas as well.

Shortly thereafter, Messiaen began to request musical scores for Christmas rather than toys. He was given several scores by Mozart, Gluck, Berlioz, and Wagner, as well as piano pieces of Debussy and Ravel. He devoured them as other children would gobble candies and cakes. These scores helped shape his fundamental musical awareness and direct the course of his own compositions. His admiration of the composers he studied greatly influenced his own creative style, although not in an imitative sense.

His first piece was written as early as age nine; it was written for the piano and was called *Le Dame de Shallot.* Of course this accomplishment was a signal to his family of things to come; however, this first piece remains unpublished. Messiaen has casually dismissed it in his interviews, calling *Le Dame de Shallot* "the mere stammering of a child."

Early Teachers

After the war, the family moved to Nantes and Messiaen met his first teachers. Jehan de Gibon, a harmony teacher, presented him with a copy of Debussy's *Pelléas et Mélisande*. In an interview with music critic Bernard Gavoty, Messiaen said, "It was an inconceivable thing in 1918 for a provincial teacher to give *Pelléas et Mélisande* to a ten-year old boy. It was this score that decided my vocation."[1]

Messiaen entered the Paris Conservatoire one year later at age eleven. He was a brilliant student, winning five Premiere Prix from the years 1926-1930—in counterpoint and fugue (1926), accompaniment (1928), organ and improvisation (1929), history of music (1929), and composition (1930).

While at the Conservatory he studied under admirable teachers: Jean Gallon, harmony; Noël Gallon, counterpoint; C. A. Estyle, piano accompaniment; George Caussade, fugue; Marcel Dupré, organ, improvisation, and plainchant; Maurice Emmanuel, history of music and Greek meter; Joseph Baggers, tympani and percussion; and Paul Dukas, composition and orchestration.

In his later writings Messiaen has consistently credited his early teachers not only for providing a thorough traditional technical background, but for stimulating his interest in new musical horizons, which he developed after leaving the conservatory. During his student years Messiaen's gifts for improvisation became evident as he began to work on what was to be his own modal system. The earliest published compositions, *Préludes pour piano* and *Le banquet céleste*, were both written during the conservatory years.

Interest in Ancient and Indian Rhythmic Patterns

Greek Rhythms

As a student at the Paris Conservatory, Messiaen began improvising with Greek rhythms on the organ with his teacher Marcel Dupré. His professor of music history, Maurice Emmanuel was an authority on Greek music and had written the chapter "Grèce" in the *Encyclopédie de la musique*.[2] Messiaen's interest in this aspect of ancient music led to his own basic philosophy and views concerning rhythm.

In ancient Greece the metric accents in both poetry and melody followed the quantitative principle; they occurred as long notes among short notes, rather than as strong beats among light beats. The short note, which we call an eighth note in modern notation, was the time unit and was called *chronos protos*. In comparison with present-day practice of successively dividing the whole note into half, quarter, and eighth notes, the Greek theory began with the *chronos protos* and by manipulations formed different rhythmic feet. The short note or *brevis* was combined with the *longa* (two *brevis* or ♩), and were classified in four groups according to ratio of length. Each type of foot that had two (equal or unequal) phases belonged to the 1:1, 2:1, 3:2, or 4:3 ratio groups. The four groups were:

1. Isa, "equals" or dactylic feet; our even-beat measures.

   Dactyl   ♩ ♫
   Anapest ♫ ♩

2. Diplasia, "doubles" or iambic feet with a ratio of 2:1.

   Iamb   ♪ ♩
   Trochée ♩ ♪

3. Hemiolia, ratio of 3:2 corresponds to our five-beat measures.

4. Epitrita, ratio of 4:3, would correspond to our seven-beat measure. These rhythms were very rare.

The *chronos protos* was usually grouped into threes, fours, fives, or sixes to form feet; the feet were grouped to form measures. All kinds of feet could be combined, into two-, three-, or four-foot units. Thus the *chronos protos* became the nucleus, which by varying combinations created larger rhythmic patterns. Some of the most common divisions of time in Greek practice may be seen in Table 1.

Table 1.   Some Greek divisions of time

Name	Ratio	*Chronos Protos*	Pattern
Anapaest	1:1	2 + 2	♫ ♩
Cretic	3:2	3 + 2	♩ ♪ ♩
Dactyl	1:1	2 + 2	♩ ♫
Iamb	1:2	1 + 2	♪ ♩
Spondée	1:1	2 + 2	♩ ♩
Tribrach	2:1	2 + 1	♫ ♪
Trochée/Chorée	2:1	2 + 1	♩ ♪

In a lecture Messiaen gave at the Conférence de Bruxelles in 1958 he said, "Let us not forget that the first, essential element in music is rhythm, and that rhythm is first, and foremost the change of number and duration. Suppose that there were a single beat in all the universe. One beat; with eternity before it and eternity after it. A before and an after. That is the birth of time. Imagine then, almost immediately, a second beat. Since any beat is prolonged in the silence which follows it, the second beat will be longer than the first. Another number, another duration. That is the birth of rhythm."[3] Thus Messiaen's philosophy regarding rhythm clearly concerns itself with the accumulation of durations rather than the division of time into equal parts. His concept of a primary time value is the underlying factor in many of his compositional techniques such as rhythmic augmentation, diminution, and chromatic rhythm. (These techniques are discussed and illustrated more fully in subsequent chapters.)

Later in his works, Messiaen developed the techniques of "permutation" and "interversions" of rhythmic patterns, also based on the primary time unit. These techniques were part of his experimental period of 1949–1951, and influenced avant-garde composers at that time (see chapts. 11 and 12).

Messiaen has identified specific Greek rhythms in the scores of works where he has included cretic patterns, for example, *Couleurs de la cité céleste* (1963) and *Sept haïkaï* (1963). These patterns sometimes occur along with other passages such as birdsong, plainchant, or Hindu rhythms. Although the primary unit of time has been the key to many of Messiaen's most distinctive stylistic techniques, the use of Greek feet is not obvious in the music of his first and second periods. The influence of Greek meters is discussed further in Chapter 10 in analyzing a movement from *Cinq rechants*.

Indian Rhythms

The influence of Indian rhythmic principles is significant in the development of Messiaen's musical language and compositional techniques. From the highly evolved traditions of the Hindustani music of northern India and of Carnatic music of southern India, the composer derived principles that led to his concepts of added values, inexact augmentation and diminution, and non-retrogradable rhythms.

To understand the derivation of Messiaen's rhythmic language, it is necessary to be familiar with some of the basic aspects of Hindu practice. It is also necessary to understand that Messiaen does not purport to be concerned with scholarly accuracy; rather, his studies provided the artistic impetus for his own techniques and concepts of composition. For example, he learned of Çarngadeva's rhythms through his study of a table given in Lavignac's *Encyclopédie de la musique et dictionnarie du composition,*[4] rather than from comprehensive study of Indian music, its ethos, and philosophies.

Çarngadeva, one of the most important Hindu theorists of the thirteenth century, wrote the most extensive system of classification of Hindu rhythmic practice in history. In his system he organized rhythm into one hundred twenty decî-tâlas, or rhythms of the Indian provinces. The table included the name of each tâla, number of matras in each tâla, the original Sanskrit notation for each pattern, and the modern transcription of each tâla. The system was derived in the following manner.

The music of India consists of two ancient systems, Hindustani music of norther India and Carnatic music of southern India. Both are organized in a manner similar to classical Greek rhythms; the Hindu system was also derived from poetic meter. The short poetic syllable is equated to a short primary time unit called a mâtra. The mâtra or time unit combines into a group of two or more time units, which repeat or combine to form two or more measures. The total pattern is called a tâla.

All tâlas do not have an equal number of mâtras, they are defined by the number of mâtras they contain in each of their divisions. Tâla is therefore a time cycle made up of a certain number of beats (mâtras), combined to achieve a total. Both Hindustani and Carnatic systems of tâla were derived in this manner.

A rhythm or tâla contains three elements: an initial beat (sama), other beats (tali), and rests (khali). In their method of notation, a sign placed over a note indicated the note's value should be prolonged by one-half.

Thus whereas Western music is organized into stressed and unstressed beats, musical time in India is a development of vocal phrasing, and percussive accent plays no part. Hindu meters are conceived as sums of a series of equal time units rather than multiples. Therefore 6/8 meter is not a pattern of multiples (2×3). Six beats might be 3 plus 1 plus 2; nine beats might be 4 plus 2 plus 3, or some other additive arrangement. The meter is therefore quantitative and melodies are organized into a rhythmical series of long and short notes.

The tâla or time scale is composed of a much larger time structure than in Western music; it would be similar to the idea of indicating in a time signature the number of measures to a phrase rather than beats to a measure.

Messiaen identifies the particular Hindu or Carnatic rhythm he uses in the scores of several of his works. Using the richness of the Hindu tradition, he assimilates into his personal style the vitality of the rhythm patterns by his development of more sophisticated practices. The most common rhythm pattern found in Messiaen's music is tâla number 93, râgavardhana: () This rhythm may be found in *Couleurs de la cité céleste, Cantéyodjavâ,* and *Le livre d'orgue.*

This rhythm may be used to serve as a model for illustrating specific rhythmic techniques, as Messiaen did in *Technique of My Musical Language,* a work that catalogues the early compositional devices.[5]

When this pattern is in retrograde form in Messiaen's music, the dotted half note is often divided into three equal shorter values.

Example 1. Ragavardhana, retrograde form

The second part of the rhythm B is a diminution of the first part A, with the addition of a half value on the second note. Messiaen thus derived the principle of added values by lengthening a note, by adding a short note value, or by adding a short rest. See illustrations of added values marked with +.

Example 2. Added values, *Technique,* Examples 7, 8, and 9

Example 1 illustrates inexact diminution. Three eighth notes would be the classic diminution of three quarter notes; the dot added to the second eighth note renders the diminution inexact. In Example 1 the fragment B also illustrates a non-retrogradable rhythm.

From this brief Hindu rhythmic pattern, Messiaen has drawn concepts that figure as a basis for his rhythmic technique:

1. Added values *(valeurs a joutées)* that transform the metric balance of any rhythm by adding small values of time

2. Forms of augmentation and diminution of rhythms, more complex than the simple classic doublings

3. Rhythms non-retrogradable, wherein the retrograde of the whole reads the same as the original

In Messiaen's musical language, the use of the short value (such as the sixteenth note and its free multiplication) produces "ametrical" music, or music with free but precise rhythmic patterns, in opposition to measured or equally barred music. Many of the passages in Messiaen's music are not barred metrically, but have barlines that serve to mark the ends of periods; the values are to be read and executed precisely as marked.

Theological Influences

Plainchant

When he left the Paris Conservatory in 1930, Messiaen was interested in exploring new means of musical expression. In 1931 he became the youngest organist in France when he was named to the post at Sainte Trinité in Paris. This position immediately provided him with an outlet for his great improvisational gifts, which eventually led to some of his best compositions.

His strong faith in Roman Catholicism as well as the position as organist in a Catholic church led to his independent studies of plainchant. This influence did not result in extensive imitation, although one can recognize it as a source of expressive melodic contours in works composed around 1933–1939.

Messiaen called plainchant an "inexhaustible mine of rare and expressive melodic contours."[6] He not only made use of these contours, but applied his technique to the forms of plainchant as well, specifically the Alleluia, Psalmody, Kyrie, and Sequence. To illuminate how Messiaen used this influence, it is necessary to describe briefly certain characteristics of plainchant and its forms.

Chants may be classified on the basis of the relationship of notes to syllables. Those in which most or all of the syllables have a single note each are called syllabic; those characterized by long melodic passages on a single syllable are called melismatic. This distinction is not always clear cut, since chants that are prevailingly melismatic usually include some syllabic sections or phrases; on the other hand, many otherwise syllabic chants have occasional short melismas of four or five notes on some syllables.

Every Gregorian melody is divided into phrases or periods that correspond to the periods of the text. These sections are marked off in modern chant books by a vertical line in the staff. In most Gregorian phrases the melodic contour takes the form of an arch; it begins low, rises to a higher pitch, where it remains for some time, then descends at the end of the phrase. The design may be worked out in a variety of combinations, but there is always subtlety of contour. The influence of this design is not always noticeable in the psalmodies and "alleluiatic vocalises"[7] that Messiaen has composed for soprano voice with piano accompaniment.

The chants for the Ordinary of the Mass were originally simple syllabic melodies; the Kyrie was arranged in a three-part sectional form:

A   Kyrie eleison

B   Christe eleison

C   Kyrie eleison

Each exclamation is uttered three times; therefore there may be an *aba* form within each of the principal sections.

A sequence is a form of chant developed between the fifth and ninth centuries. It is essentially an addition of words and music to an established liturgical chant, most likely originating with the alleluias of the Proper of the Mass.

Messiaen uses the original forms of the plainchant in a variety of ways. For example, he might retain a form of plainchant in one melodic line, while superimposing another vocal line, and then surrounding this music with a quasi-atonal counterpoint.[8] The alleluiatic vocalise, which Messiaen considers to be the most essential part of the alleluia, is retained and blended with psalmody (wherein the words are uttered at a very rapid pace on a repeated note). So that he could adopt his own system of declamation by blending plainchant techniques of alleluiatic vocalise with psalmody, Messiaen preferred to write his own lyrics.

For example, in *Poèmes pour Mi,* Part I, "Action de grâces" and Part VIII, "Prière exaucée," Messiaen endeavors to arrive at a vocal text that imitates the inflections of speech, while also allowing the voice the freedom to sing. He achieves this by adopting two plainchant techniques: what is in the domain of recitative he writes as psalmody, or in the manner of syllabic chant in which the words are uttered rapidly on a repeated note; and any especially important word rich in meaning is adorned with a long or even very long vocalise.

An example of a more sophisticated form of the Kyrie may be found in the organ piece, *Les corps glorieux,* Part VII, *Meditations sur le Mystère de la Sainte Trinité,* where the pattern was *ABC* with smaller *aba* form in each section. In Part *C* the last repetition of the initial phrases includes expansion and melodic conclusion. This piece in triparte form, which has been derived in form from plainchant, is written in three voices and uses some highly recognizable twentieth-century techniques in its texture.

Messiaen uses the sequence form in his organ work, *La nativité du Seigneur,* Part IV, "Le verbe," in which he combines a variety of other original compositional techniques. Thus we find repeatedly the influence of plainchant as part of the synthesis of elements that interweave to become Messiaen's style.

Messiaen states in Volume 1 of *Technique* that in making use of plainchant he ignores their rhythms and their modes.[9] In 1949, however, five years after *Technique* was published, he did use rhythmic neumes[10] extensively in "Neumes rhythmiques."

Although Messiaen's early paraphrasing of chant in the 1930s was more elaborate rhythmically than the original, in later works his use of this material tends to be rhythmically simple, probably to ensure that the chant remains recognizable. Indeed, with respect to his highly developed and complicated rhythmic practice, the chant paraphrases in his later music appear unusual in simplicity.

Works that contain paraphrases of chants include *Quatuor pour la fin du temps* (1941), "Vocalise, pour l'Ange qui annonce la fin du temps"; *Vingt regards sur l'Enfant Jésus* (1944), "Premiere communion" and "Regard de l'esprit."

In the 1960s Messiaen included paraphrases of several plainchant alleluias in *Verset pour la fête de la dédicace* (1960), *Couleurs de la cité céleste* (1964) and *Et exspecto resurrectionem mortuorum* (1964).

In his scores, Messiaen identifies the original plainchant his music paraphrases. These Gregorian plainchants may be found in *The Liber Usualis*[11] and can be compared with Messiaen's usage of them in his works.

Spiritual Development

Regardless of how completely one studies the influences that became synthesized into Messiaen's style, an understanding of his music would be deficient without some awareness of his psychological makeup and his spiritual inspiration. Authors and critics who have thoroughly studied his music are aware of this. Norman Demuth says, "To appreciate Messiaen's music to its fullest extent, a certain degree of sympathy with his philosophy is necessary, and to understand the philosophy is to understand the music, for the two are inextricably intertwined. This is more pertinent with Messiaen than with most other composers."[12]

Messiaen describes his musical intent as completely intertwined with his faith: "God being present in all things, music dealing with theological subjects can and must be extremely varied . . . I have therefore, in the words of Ernest Hello [surrealist poet], tried to produce a music that touches all things without ceasing to touch God'"[13] In his conversations with Claude Samuel, Messiaen elaborates further on the importance of the Catholic faith. He speaks of human love and the love of nature not as being opposed to faith in God, but as being complementary to it and implied in it. Concerning human love, or the Tristan myth, Messiaen says, "A great love is a reflection, a pale reflection, but nevertheless a reflection of the one true love, the divine love."[14]

Although certain movements of Messiaen's music have a mystical meaning and tend toward a mystical expression within the theological framework, he describes his thought as being theological rather than mystical. The controversy about these two conceptions as attributed to Messiaen's philosophy became most blatant in the middle 1940s when his music reflected not only religious themes, but turned to themes of human love and death. Messiaen clarified these views further in *Entretiens* by referring to nature as God's creation, a "manifestation of the divine." He therefore relates the three aspects of his work and inspiration, namely, the Catholic faith, nature, and human love as being united in one and the same idea: divine love. Certain critics have resented his blending of religious themes with passionate human love; others have called into question the attribution of mystical qualities to the composer.

There is a precise difference between mysticism and theology and that difference is of great importance. Francis Routh defines mysticism as "a state of mind in which by contemplation, a man seeks to reach outside and beyond the confines of his human state, and thus experience contact with the Divinity." Theology is according to Routh "the science of religion and is concerned with the human condition," with God's act of redemption in the world, with the function of "reconciling the imperfections of this world with the Divine glory." Routh also says that this later aim is the sole purpose of Messiaen's creative thought: "He first interprets theologically a visionary or mystical theme; he then expresses this poetically in its different aspects, so as to give a series of ideas, or pictures which will make a framework for the movements, or sections of a composition."[15] The arguments about Messiaen's spiritual influences and philosophical grounding are merely a side issue, however, when one considers the indisputability of his thorough musicianship.

His musical means of theological interpretation are not at cross-purposes with other influences, such as Symbolism or the surrealism of his favorite poet. On the contrary, the importance of symbolism in the Catholic religion is related to all the articles of faith.

In many works he makes use of cyclic themes that have a symbolic function within the context of the work in which they appear (see the discussion of *Vingt regards,* chapt. 8).

Certain keys in association with specific modes of limited transposition are also associated with symbolic ideas. For example, the key of F-sharp major, together with mode 2 has been associated often with expressing the mystical experience of a superhuman love; it is used in several of Messiaen's works in slow ecstatic movements (see the discussion of *Prélude No. 2,* chapt. 3). The key of E major in slow movements has been symbolically associated with the praise of the Blessed Trinity. The "Louange à l'eternité de Jésus" and "Louange à l'immortalité de Jésus" from *Quatuor* would be examples of this.

Like the theologians of the Middle Ages, Messiaen attaches symbolic importance to certain numbers. This is often stated in the preface to a specific work, for example, *Quatuor* (see chapt. 7).

In chapter 2, section 1 of *Technique,* Messiaen discusses ametrical music and his "predilection for the rhythms of prime numbers (five, seven, eleven, thirteen)." This symbolic association with numbers provides the strong tie that makes the connection to his use of Greek and Hindu rhythm patterns.

In his more recent works, a source of symbolism has been some of the meanings of the Çàrngadeva rhythms that he has used since *La nativité du Seigneur* (1935) at the beginning of his second creative period. This indicates that over the years he has chosen to pursue a more comprehensive study of Indian philosophy and its rhythms.

Influence of Other Composers

Fourteenth-century Isorhythm

In his book, *Rhythm and Tempo,* Curt Sachs indicates that the fourteenth century, or the French gothic age, was probably a period of influence for Messiaen.[16] Techniques that are predominant in his music were in the French spirit of writing around 1400. These include specifically canonic devices such as:

1. Actual rhythmic canon in stretto at the distance of a quarter note

2. Augmentation and diminution, exact or approximate, of the constituent values of a rhythmic pattern

3. Crab canon, where not the melodic steps, but individual time values going backward from end to middle of the piece correspond to those that go from the beginning forward to the middle

Among Western composers, Machaut (d. 1377) used isorhythmic organization in the majority of his motets.[17]

Messiaen's technique of rhythmic pedal or "rhythm which repeats itself indefatigably, in ostinato"[18] functions independently of melodic or harmonic demands and often continues for extended periods.

When more than one isorhythmic part appeared simultaneously, the context used by Willi Apel is panisorhythm.[19] This type of organization was followed in the fifteenth century, and appears in two works by Messiaen: the first movements of both *Quatuor pour la fin du temps* and the *Turangalîla-symphonie*. (See analysis of "Liturgie de cristal" from *Quatuor*, in chapt. 7.)

Messiaen has mentioned Alban Berg as being influential in the development of his style and it is likely that he was aware of Berg's use of rhythm as an element independent of melody in *Wozzeck*. Both composers may have been consciously unaware of techniques in isorhythm used in the fourteenth century when they were developing their own techniques of composition. Regarding the use of two superimposed independent rhythmic pedals (panisorhythm) in *Quatuor*, Robert Sherlaw Johnson says, "Messiaen himself emphasizes the importance of the dissociation of rhythm from harmony and melody in this work 'in the manner of Guillaume de Machaut whose work I did not know at the time.'"[20]

Influence of Debussy

At the beginning of the twentieth century, a number of different trends in music began to evolve. Collaer, in listing four "generations" of musicians, places Claude Debussy in the first generation, Stravinsky in the second, and Messiaen in the third.[21] He also describes phases of discovery, for example, phase 1 (1909–1923), a period of harmonic and rhythmic discovery and of spiritual and technical liberation; phase 2 (1923–1940), a period when form takes a new spotlight while the freedom acquired in the first phase is prudently exercised; phase 3 (since 1940), a period of extension of musical knowledge to very old periods and distant lands, of which Messiaen's explorations are examples.

During this time there was no universal technique, no so-called schools existed. The diversity in techniques corresponded to diversity in personal style, and there were leaders who guided and attracted disciples. Two divergent trends stand out as being of great importance in view of later musical developments. One was represented by the serialism of the second Viennese school, while another, represented by Debussy and Stravinsky, was firmly opposed to the excesses of the late nineteenth century and its grandiose conception of the role of the symphony. Messiaen's philosophy and musical language, although based on a thorough grounding in traditional form and harmony, directed his evolution to the latter path. From Debussy he inherited the coloristic rather than the traditional (directional) conception of harmony. This led him to rethink the relationships between pitch organization and rhythm. His predilection for color (both in harmony and instrumental timbres) was doubtlessly nurtured by Debussy and the works of his own teacher Paul Dukas during the post-Impressionism phase. While both Debussy and Messiaen cultivated modal harmonics, Messiaen invented his own modes[22] (see chapt. 2). The harmonic and melodic color derived from these "modes of limited transposition" are, however, part of the elements that make Messiaen's music his own. In his interviews with Claude Samuel, Messiaen commented that the color of his music corresponds more to that of Paul Dukas than to that of Debussy. Regarding his method of composition Messiaen says, "I try to convey colors through the music; certain combinations of tones and certain sonorities are bound to certain color combinations, and I employ them to this end."[23]

Debussy objected to the term Impressionsim as applied to his style of writing. As it is derived from the school of painting, it implies that Debussy set out to portray a landscape, and this is not exclusively so. Francis Routh, in his discussion of influential areas of Debussy on twentieth-century composers, believes that Debussy's esthetic as well as his style is more accurately referred to in terms of symbolism.[24] The Symbolist movement in literature formed the esthetic in Debussy's style up to and including *Pelléas et Mélisande* (1902), the work which was the major influence on Messiaen's development as a composer.

Debussy was a friend and admirer of symbolist poets such as Mallarmé. Messiaen says, "I have been a great reader and admirer of Pierre Reverdy and Paul Eluard. I am, therefore, some sort of surrealist in the poems for my works."[25]

In the sense that both composers use symbolism, or literary and poetic ideas for musical inspiration but primarily for the purpose of illuminating the entire piece, the approach to harmony and to form was influenced or affected in a similar manner. When Debussy and Messiaen began to develop larger pieces, they did not rely on the developmental processes of the previous century. Rather, the large form is an accumulation of smaller units, yet not merely an arbitrary juxtaposition of unrelated ideas. The structure results from a continuing thought process that produces a series of related images.

The two composers used similar harmonic processes, but produced dissimilar sonorities: Debussy used the whole-tone scale; Messiaen avoided it, composing primarily with his invented modes, which are limited, as is the whole-tone scale. The limited nature of these scales produced the essentially static effect that is common to the music of both.

The nondeveloping nature of Messiaen's music is derived from his philosophical intent to suspend the sense of time in music in order to express the idea of the eternal (in which time does not exist), as distinct from the temporal. To achieve this effect, Messiaen views harmony as a static element.

Other facets of his use of harmony that he attributes to Debussy are added notes such as the added sixth and augmented fourth. Also, music written during Messiaen's early period contains many examples of eleventh and thirteenth chords without resolution, which were developed by Ravel during the post-Impressionism phase.

Messiaen was again Debussy's successor in that he made rhythm independent of the melody and harmony. A history of twenthieth-century music reveals this gradual disassociation of the rhythmic element, the revolt against the barline that began with Beethoven and Brahms and continued with Debussy and Stravinsky. Debussy, by varying subdivisions of the beat between duple and triple, and by frequent ties over the barline, destroyed any regular metric grouping. Messiaen's slow rhythmic and harmonic movement in his early period may also reflect Debussy's influence, that is, the concentration on what *is*, or the total reality of the present moment, which Debussy achieved by an uncertainty of progression.

To summarize the influences of Debussy, therefore, one can see asymmetrical patterns and the abolishment of meter as two of the techniques employed by Messiaen. In the area of harmony are Debussy's added notes such as the added sixth and augmented fourth; and Debussy's coloristic concept certainly inspired Messiaen.

Antoine Golea describes Debussy's precursor role as a "starting point of the revolution in the musical language of our time." He considerd Messiaen the next important link in revolutionary mutations: "Twenty years after Debussy's death, Messiaen, in the first phase of his creative activity, had only incomparably enlarged and systematized Debussy's gains. Messiaen went on to universalize Debussy's modal message . . . to them he would add modes of his own invention, which answered to the most precise definitions, but did not however prevent the flowering of one of the most abundant melodic inspirations of our century."[26]

Stravinsky and Russian Music

The asymmetrical characteristic of duration occurring in many of Messiaen's phrases and rhythmic patterns exists in all of his creative periods because he has always believed that only asymmetrical movement is rhythmic. In *Entretiens,* he says that rhythmic music is inspired by the movements in nature, which have free and inequal durations.[27] Based on the argument that rhythmic music scorns equal divisions, Messiaen selected Stravinsky's *Le sacre du printemps* as an example of rhythmic writing. Later, when he became a professor of harmony at Paris Conservatoire, his analysis of that work was so detailed that it required a full year of study to complete. This is probably the most significant study of Stravinsky's rhythmic practices. An account of Messiaen's analysis is presented by one of his students, Jean Barraque, in "Rythme et developpement."[28] Pierre Boulez's analysis of *Sacre,* derived from the analytical study in Messiaen's classes, may be found in *Notes of an Apprenticeship.*[29]

The influence of Stravinsky on Messiaen's compositions certainly stems from his early masterpiece. Stravinsky's ostinatos, his rhythmic themes, forceful irregular accents, and asymmetrical groupings in *Sacre* are important areas of study for the serious music student.

Messiaen claims that his technique of *personnages rythmiques* is derived from the expansion and contraction of rhythmic cells in *Sacre,* especially the "Danse sacrale" and "Glorification de l'ilue." Messiaen illustrates this Volume 2 of *Technique* with a fragment from "Danse sacrale,"[30] and subsequently with the Hindu rhythm simhavikridita.[31]

In Example 3 there is diminution of A at the plus sign; B does not change.

Example 3. *Le sacre du printemps,* "Danse sacrale"

Extract from *Le sacre du printemps* by Igor Stravinsky. Example 1 of Messiaen's *Technique,* published by Alphonse Leduc & Cie., Paris, France.

The progressive augmentation or diminution of values or rhythmic cells had already become one of Messiaen's techniques. Upon noticing the tripartite organization of rhythmic cells in "Danse sacrale," he related it to living material, which accounts for his describing it as *personnages rhythmique*. This association probably developed from his early theatrical background, although he did not use it to create music for opera or theatrical situations. The concept of *personnages rhythmique* he describes in *Conférence de Bruxelles*:

Imagine a stage: three characters are on the floor; the first is active, he controls the scene; the second is moved by the first, the third is present without taking part in the conflict; he watches and does not move. In the same way, three rhythmic groups are facing each other; the first is in augmentation; the second is in diminution, the person attacked; the third never changes, the motionless person. In the fifth movement of my *Turangalîla-symphonie*, I have used a development of six rhythmic entities. Two are in augmentation, two in diminution, and two remain unchanged. [32]

Works in which this technique appear are *Turangalîla-symphonie*, *Messe de la Pentecôte*, and *Le livre d'orgue*. Although the basic idea derives from Stravinsky, the term, the explanation, and development of the technique belong to Messiaen's creative imagination.

Examples of ostinato occuring in Stravinsky's music may be found in both *Sacre* and symphony of Psalms. This technique of repeated pattern Messiaen calls rhythmic pedal.

Messiaen also assimilated other practices of Stravinksy's *Sacre* into his own language, for example, techniques which obscure metrical regularity. Polyrhythmic layers and development of rhythmic units by a variety of manipulations are two such practices.

In chapter 8 on melody in *Technique*, Messiaen credits old French songs and especially Russian folklore with remarkable melodies. He illustrates the practice of "passing them through the deforming prism of our language" by examples in Volume 2. [33] The melodic contours of passages from Moussorgsky's *Boris Godounov* and Grieg's *Chanson de Solveig* also serve as models of inspiration to Messiaen. He illustrates in this chapter his means of drawing the essence from selected melodic fragments as he transforms them into his own music. These composers from the nationalist group (Grieg) as well as the Russian Five (Moussorgsky) contributed to the heritage of Debussy, Stravinksy, and, in turn, Messiaen. The score of *Boris Godounov* had made its way from Russia to France and served as inspiration to the French with its rhythmic and harmonic freedom. The unresolved dissonance, additive rhythms, modal melodies, frequent meter changes, pedal points, ostinatos, and means of achieving colorful orchestral sonorities are techniques that very likely reinforced as well as inspired the development of Messiaen's complex individual style.

La Jeune France

In 1936 Messiaen helped organize the group *La Jeune France,* which consisted of himself, Yves Baudrier, André Jolivet, and Daniel Lesur. Messiaen had recently begun his first teaching positions at both the Schola Cantorum and the Ecole Normale de Musique. His first marriage to violinist Claire Delbos had also taken place, and his son Pascal was born the following year.

At this time the desire for simplicity and balance in musical expression had resulted in the development of neoclassicism. Members of *La Jeune France* opposed this trend; Messiaen himself believed that neoclassicism was a backward move in the evolution of music. Moreover, the group felt that technique had become an end in itself to the neoclassicist; they preferred to be inspired by humanistic values. For these reasons, *La Jeune France* was considered to be avant-garde.

The unity of the group was engendered from the members' general aspirations, which were esthetic in nature. A manifesto stating their creed was printed in the program of their first concert, which took place at Salle Gaveau in Paris on June 3, 1936. The manifesto reads:

As the conditions of life become more and more hard, mechanical and impersonal, music must bring ceaselessly to those who live it its spiritual violence and its courageous reactions. *La Jeune France,* reaffirming the title once created by Berlioz, pursues the road upon which the master once took his obdurate course. This is a friendly group of four young composers: Olivier Messiaen, Daniel Lesure, Yves Baudrier, and Andre Jolivet. *La Jeune France* proposes the dissemination of works youthful, free, as far removed from revolutionary formulas as from academic formulas. . . .

The tendencies of this group will be diverse: their only unqualified agreement is in the common desire to be satisfied with nothing less than sincerity, generosity and artistic good faith. Their aim is to create and to promote a living music. . . .[34]

It was the intention of the group to focus on musical humanism, the personal aspects of man, rather than emphasize technique in the abstract, intellectual manner. The four composers were unanimously celebrated by critics who called them "leaders of that current of lofty thought which enjoyably regenerates young French music."[35]

Although they were in agreement on purpose, they did not totally agree on how to achieve their ideals. When the war struck France in 1939, the brief life of *La Jeune France* ended.

Messiaen as Educator

After the war, in 1942, Messiaen was appointed Professor of Harmony at the Paris Conservatoire. The following year he began private classes in composition at the home of Guy Bernard-Delapierre. Some of his most illustrious pupils came to the classes: Pierre Boulez, Yvonne Loriod, Karlheinz Stockhausen, and Serge Nigg. In 1947 the director of the Conservatorie, Claude Delvincourt, hoping to avoid controversy among more senior faculty members in the area of composition, appointed Messiaen as Professor of Analysis, Aesthetics, and Rhythm. This was to be a special position that would not offend the faculty of composition, who had many years of seniority. This class became, in essence, however, a composition class, attracting outstanding students from around the world. Messiaen's official appointment as Professor of Composition at the Conservatory finally resulted nearly twenty years later, in 1966.

To answer the questions of his first eager students, Messiaen wrote the didactic *Technique de mon langage musical* in 1944, which covered his compositional techniques until that time. Volume 1 contains the text and Volume 2 the musical examples. This work is not a treatise on his compositions, but does list his early devices. It does not purport to represent the Messiaen of today, who has never ceased to move on to newer phases of creativity.

Messiaen's importance as a teacher, his open-mindedness and ability to guide the talents of his brilliant avant-garde pupils resulted in his being the direct influence on the course of postwar European music. Thus as teacher and composer his reputation was firmly established.

During the 1940s Messiaen found a superb interpreter of his piano music in his pupil Yvonne Loriod, and was inspired to write his major works for piano *(Visions de l'Amen, Vingt regards sur l'Enfant Jésus)*. Miss Loriod has since performed his music with brilliant technique and sensitivity in concerts all over the world. Their association of twenty years resulted in marriage in 1962, following the death of Messiaen's first wife in 1959 after a long and tragic illness.

Total Organization

As an innovator, Messiaen is perhaps best known for composing the first work of so-called total organization, "Mode de valeurs et d'intensitiés," from the *Quatre études de rythme* (1949). In a piece that is "totally organized" the performer can take no liberties with the speed or intensity (volume) of the music. The composer indicates the exact duration of each note as well as the exact intensity of each tone. This method of composition is a form of serialism that goes beyond the earlier twelve-note principle of Harold Schoenberg. Whereas Schoenberg controlled the order of tones, Messiaen controlled the duration, timbre, and intensity as well. Thus Messiaen found the ultimate implications of serial music, which was not accomplished by the twelve-tone system. His "discovery" became the point of departure for all avant-garde composers during the 1950s and 1960s. He had provided a link in the evolution of music that opened up infinite new possibilities.

Lover of Nature and Birdsong

One cannot discuss the music of Olivier Messiaen without including the influence of birdsong. As a youth, he instinctively had made attempts to notate birdsong; his research of birds has since been a lifelong endeavor. Melodies with the characteristics of bird style first appeared in *Quatuor* ("Liturgie de cristal"; see chapt. 7), and became the exclusive basis of works written in the 1950s: *Reveil des oiseaux* (1953), *Oiseaux exotiques* (1956), and *Catalogue d'oiseaux* (1956–1958).

Johnson describes *Catalogue d'oiseaux* as "Messiaen's most important work of his birdsong period and possibly his greatest piano work."[36] (See chapt. 12 for analysis of Part V, "La chouette hulotte.")

Messiaen's interest in birdsong stems from his love of nature, to which he turns for spiritual strength as well as for inspiration. He has said that he often returns to nature to seek out the true lost face of music somewhere among the birds in the forest, in the fields, in the mountains, or on the seashore.

Messiaen has also said that birdsong has renewed his birthright as a musician. In the *Conférence de Bruxelles* (13) written in 1958, he said, "But inspiration is not the fruit of will. When all seems lost, when the way is no longer clear, to what master can one turn? In the face of so many opposing schools and contradictory languages, there is no human music to restore confidence to the desperate. This is where the voices of nature intervene."

How can it be explained that they have been overlooked by so many musicians, while painters and poets have always sought lessons from them?"

As was stated previously with regard to his use of Hindu rhythms and plainchant, Messiaen often identifies in the score of a work the specific bird that is being quoted or "paraphrased."

The use of birdsong is discussed briefly in *Technique,* although this work was written prior to Messiaen's most significant compositions using this technique. Over the years 1941–1953, he became an amateur ornithologist and has continued to spend much time studying birds in their native environment. In relating the difficulties of making accurate transcriptions of their songs, Messiaen said, "The bird sings in extremely quick tempi which are absolutely impossible for our instruments; I am therefore obliged to transcribe the song at a slower tempo. In addition, this rapidity is allied to an extreme acuteness, the bird being able to sing in excessively high registers which are inaccessible to our instruments; I transcribe the song, therefore, one, two, three, or even four octaves lower. For the same reasons, I am obliged to suppress the very small intervals which our instruments cannot play, but I respect the scale of values between the different intervals."[37] Thus these passages are constructed according to the tenet of, or in an attempt at authentic reproduction of, the song of the bird.

Trevor Hold has done a detailed study of the authenticity of the use of birdsong in Messiaen's music.[38] Although this study is too detailed to elaborate on here, it involved the comparison of Messiaen's quotations to birdsong that was notated from a sound-spectrograph. The results of Hold's study indicate that Messiaen uses a type of paraphrase rather than authentic reproduction, although he admitted that the composer succeeded in reproducing certain salient features, such as patterns of short ostinato phrases, the superimposition of contrasting strata of sound, and in certain cases, the basic shape of a song. While critics of Messiaen debate on whether the birdsong is authentic transcription or transmutations, most concur that this music contains many moments that are beautiful and imaginative.

Messiaen, the Cosmopolitan

During the 1960s and 1970s Messiaen has been on the move constantly, performing his music worldwide, usually in concert with Yvonne Loriod. Many of these performances have been world premieres; other appearances have been as lecturer or recipient of honors. Messiaen's music has a universal quality, and his followers at New York City concerts border on cultists. His audience grows as more and more people respond to the dynamic and highly unique style of his music; as their ears become attuned to the masterful blend of sonorities, techniques, and inspirational feelings that ultimately become the music of Olivier Messiaen.

2

The Musical Language

To understand Messiaen's development as a composer, we must remember that, although his training at the Paris Conservatory was complete in its study of traditional musical forms, his direction was not in the nineteenth-century symphonic tradition. He made creative choices with a confidence derived from a highly disciplined technique and from his own intentions. His style grew directly from a concept that includes a wide musical and cultural background, spiritual and philosophical beliefs, related musical ideas, and his own means of expression. In his desire to express the timelessness of the universe, he creates a harmony existing in a state that is neither tension nor relaxation in a structure that does not seek progressions based on a principle of dissonance and resolution.

Messiaen attempts to express in sound the images inspired by his faith in God and in the Roman Catholic Church. The result is often a structure based on sectional form rather than on traditional thematic development. As the forms become larger the structure continues to be an accumulation of smaller units. The process connecting the music stems from the images Messiaen often describes in regard to each work. Therefore his musical structure usually conveys a logical and continuing thought process very often descriptive of events, miracles, or holy images inherent in Roman Catholicism.

In surveying his prolific output, it is evident that modifications in style evolve from the techniques formulated in early years and developed gradually. No sharp cleavage is evident from one period to the next; however, it is logical and practical to group Messiaen's works into three general periods. The first period extends from 1928 *(Le banquet céleste)* through 1934 *(L'ascension),* and includes works that reveal his traditional musical background and technical competence as well as the fundamentals of his individualistic art.

For the following fifteen years, Messiaen extended his techniques through musical explorations, most particularly in the field of rhythm. Midway through this second period he wrote *The Technique of My Musical Language*.[1] With the writing of the *Turangalîla-symphonie* in 1948 his creative development culminated. Changes of direction that Messiaen had forecasted are found in later compositions.

From 1949–1951 and on to the present time is the third, often labeled the experimental, period; one can see that it covers a larger time span than previous groupings. This era contains works that reflect the entire evolution of Messiaen's musical language. Notable is his employment of serialism. Although Messiaen continued to use certain facets of this technique, which has subsequently influenced many contemporary composers, he also returned to his preferred religious images and nature for inspiration and for expression of his music.

In an analysis of his music, it is necessary to understand the makeup of his total esthetic vision. This requires an evaluation according to new principles that are relevant to determining Messiaen's purposes, rather than one that invites comparison with previously established criteria for works having entirely different goals.

Messiaen's music consistently uses a modal or polymodal form based on our present chromatic system, a tempered system of twelve sounds. Invented by Messiaen, and named the "modes of limited transposition," the modes are explained briefly by the composer in chapter 16 of *Technique* (1:58–63). Of chief importance is the wide variety of harmonic color provided by the modes; however, they form the basis of melody as well. Each mode divides the octave into two, three, or four equal intervals. Each interval then subdivides into an identical relationship of tones and semitones.

Mode 1 consists of the whole-tone scale and separates the octave into six equal divisions. Messiaen considers that Debussy "made such remarkable use of it that there is nothing to add."[2] He therefore uses it rarely, unless it is well concealed in a superimposition of modes. Modes 1 through 7 of limited transposition are shown in Example 4.[3]

Example 4. Modes of limited transposition

Mode 1

Mode 2, first transposition

Mode 3, first transposition

Mode 4, first transposition

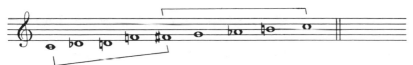

Mode 5, first transposition

Mode 6, first transposition

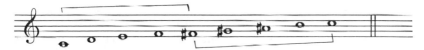

Mode 7, first transposition

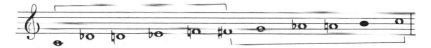

The basic position of each mode, starting on C, is the first transposition. Mode 2 is transposable three times (starting the pattern on C, C-sharp, and D); the fourth transposition, starting on E-flat, would give exactly the same notes as the first (see Example 5). It is important to remember that enharmonics are interchangeable. Mode 3 is transposable four times.

The last four modes, each transposable six times, appear less frequently because he prefers the limits delegated by modes 2 and 3 with fewer transpositions. In Chapter 1 of *Technique* he refers to this limitation as "the

Example 5. Mode 2

First transposition

Fourth transposition, beginning on E-flat

charm of impossibilites" and relates this concept to both harmonic and rhythmic musical thought (1:13).

The modes of Messiaen's music based on logical harmonic thought result in a consistent system. It is mathematically impossible to find other modes that follow the structural laws inherent in these.[4] They are dissimilar to Indian, ancient Greek, and Chinese modes, and to plainchant. Messiaen has stated that "they are in the atmosphere of several tonalities at once, without polytonality, the composer being free to give predominance to one of the tonalities or to leave the tonal impression unsettled."[5]

The modes can modulate to themselves or borrow from themselves in their different transpositions; they can alternate; they can modulate to another mode; they can combine to produce polymodality. The modes led Messiaen to an extended tonality and finally to a total chromaticism or pantonality. Since pantonality, a state inclusive of all tonalities, is impossible to achieve,[6] it is similar to the semicontradictory expression, "abandonment of tonality."

One of the most fundamental aspects of Messiaen's harmonic vocabulary is the principle of notes added to simple chords. He adds the sixth, seventh, and ninth, as well as the interval of the augmented fourth (tritone), which he states can be heard in the resonance of a given tone as the eleventh harmonic.[7]

In another procedure Messiaen uses the appoggiatura in forming the "chord on the dominant." He considers this accented dissonance to have "citizenship in the chord," and by adding further appoggiaturas creates a chord that now combines both dissonance and resolution[8] (see Example 6).

Melodically, Messiaen's style has a certain correspondence to his use of harmony in that he favors specific intervals, which appear in melodic

Example 6. Chord on the dominant and resolution

contours as well as in chords. Two of his favored intervals are the tritone
and the descending major sixth. These and other melodic features will also
be pointed out as they occur as being characteristic of Messiaen's style.

In his book *Technique* Messiaen places rhythmic considerations first in
sequential order. It is obvious that rhythm has been his primary occupa-
tion, even though he gives supremacy to melody. The basic rhythmic
principles of added values, augmentation and diminution, and non-
retrogradable rhythms originate with Hindu rhythm. These most important devices in Messiaen's compositions are explained within the
framework of the specific musical selections. The use of Greek rhythms is
not obvious during the first period of Messiaen's music, but becomes more
noticeable during the latter part of the second period.

Messiaen compares polyrhythm, resulting from the imposition of one
independent rhythm on another, to the superimposition of modes upon one
another (see *Technique* 1:13). The devices of panisorhythm, chromatic
rhythm, and rhythmic pedal, which result in polyrhythm, gain definition in
the analysis.

In the music discussed in chapters 3 through 8 (or of the first and second
periods), melodic rather than harmonic considerations generate the forms
since the harmony is primarily coloristic rather than structural. Messiaen
cites three basic forms (1:37–38) that he considers characteristic of his
work to that time. Descriptions of these as well as his definition of theme
and commentary follow.

> Theme—a synthesis of the elements in the song sentence
> (usually the first period).

> Commentary—a melodic development of a theme in which
> fragments are repeated on different degrees and varied
> rhythmically, melodically, and harmonically. Elements
> that are foreign to the theme may also be developed,
> provided they are similar to the theme in style.

Song sentence—a succession of periods that are usually divided this way:

    a. Theme (antecedent and consequent)
    b. Middle period, often inflected toward the dominant
    c. Final period, an issue of the theme

Binary sentence—a sentence that is divided as follows:

    a. Theme
    b. First commentary (modulating more or less, inflected toward the dominant of initial key)
    c. Theme
    d. Second commentary (concluding on the tonic of the original key)

Ternary sentence—a musical sentence that is divided thus:

    a. Theme
    a'. Consequent of theme
    b. Commentary
    b'. Consequent of the commentary
    c. Theme
    c'. Consequent of the theme

Formal discussions in this analysis correspond as much as possible to Messiaen's terminology for form.

Another consideration relates to Messiaen's methods of notating his music. In *Technique* (1:28–30), he identifies four types of notation that he uses. These are appropriate to the analysis of his music, although they do not include all of the practices in contemporary music notation, nor do they include his manner of notation when he is writing in the style of birds.

1. First notation represents the exact expression of the composer. It consists of writing the exact values without time signature or beat. The barline is used to indicate phrases, periods, and to cancel the effects of accidentals, but not to indicate a regular meter. This method is excellent for one soloist or for small ensemble.[9]

2. Second notation resembles traditional barring and explains the many metric variations with time signature changes. This is most similar to conventional notation and is for use with complex scores, thus avoiding the difficulty in reading a score written in first notation for a large ensemble. *Cinq*

rechants, written in this type of notation, includes many changes of meter.

3. For different rhythms such as those in *Poèmes pour Mi* for voice and orchestra, Messiaen uses a third notation developed by Roger Desormiere, in which signs appear over note values to indicate their true duration. A number written at the head of each measure indicates the number of beats in that measure.

4. In the fourth type of notation, the composer uses a normal meter, and writes a rhythm that has no relation to it. The barlines accommodate the performer; the listener hears the true meter by means of accent marks placed by the composer where he actually intends them. This system is necessary when several musicians are performing different rhythms that are complicated. The piano part in "Louange a l'eternité de Jésus" *(Quatuor)* or the clarinet part in "Liturgie de cristal" *(Quatuor)* provide good examples of fourth notation as used by Messiaen.

To conclude this discussion of musical language, we consider the role played by color in Messiaen's works. Although the use of color is not visible in his music as a technique, its reality for Messiaen played a large part in the craft of his compositions.

When reading a score, or listening to music, Messiaen has always had the unusual reaction of seeing color impressions that vary according to the sonorities and timbres. Visual impressions, as well, transform themselves into music or suggest melodies to him, which correspond to a format of colors. This phenomenon, which science calls synesthesia, or the simultaneous impression of color and sound, developed further when Messiaen was a prisoner during the Second World War.

Through the use of the harmonic modes, which are limited to a certain number of transpositions and which draw their special coloration from that fact, Messiaen states that he succeeded in "putting wheels of color in opposition, into interweaving rainbows, finding complementary colors in music."[10] By the selection of a particular mode, Messiaen is able to achieve the type of melodic and harmonic "picture" he desires:

I attempt, in effect, to convey colors through the music; certain combinations of tones and certain sonorities are bound to certain color combinations, it seems to me, and in the knowledge of this, I employ the tones and sonorities to this end.[11]

Messiaen has described liberally the exact colors that each mode suggests to him:

Mode 1—reddish-violet

Mode 3—orange in a halo of milky white, speckled with a little red like an opal

Mode 4—dark purple

Mode 5—gray-pink-green dotted with gold

Chords on the dominant--prussian blue spotted with red, gold, orange, and lilac[12]

Messiaen spoke of modal colors throughout the 1940s; during the 1950s he concentrated more on the use of birdsong. His concerns with color returned with *Chronochromie* (1960); he used color in a number of ways in major works through 1969, including rhythmic and serially derived colors. Although the phenomenon of synesthesia is not accessible to most of us, knowledge of Messiaen's simultaneous use of sound and color provides insight into his compositions.

Many of the materials that provide the basic elements of Messiaen's musical language were clearly defined when he wrote his first published pieces, *Le banquet céleste* (1928) and the eight *Préludes pour piano* (1929). These include the modes of limited transposition; added notes to harmony, such as the sixth and the augmented fourth; and rhythmic practices such as augmentation and diminution. The non-retrogradable rhythms fascinated Messiaen because of their limitations, as did the modes of limited transposition. Other rhythmic practices such as the added value, augmentation, and diminution were soon to follow. Elements of his craft such as the structural form, manner of notation, early harmonic practices, and use of sound-color are part of the musical language with which he created his earliest compositions, and he has continued to develop and expand this musical vocabulary throughout his career.

3

Piano Prelude No. 2 (1929)

Messiaen continued his studies at the Paris Conservatory from 1919 until 1930. In the beginning of his study, his performing instrument was the piano. It continued to be his favorite instrument for composing, even though he had developed a formidable technique on the organ, which at that time was the instrument most associated with improvisation; this explains Messiaen's desire to learn the instrument.

During this time Messiaen's interests were developing along lines that proved crucial to his stylistic development. Principally, these were Greek rhythms, birdsong, and the table of one hundred twenty Indian decî-tâla, to which was added the influence of his professors Emmanuel and Dupré. Although he began to explore facets of rhythmic techniques at this time, these elements did not appear in such early works as the prelude described in this chapter.

While these techniques were being touched on, in one area Messiaen had already achieved his true identity. What he did consider himself to be at this time, was a sound-color composer. He had already invented his own modal system that had come to fruition through improvisation in the class taught by Dupré. This system, modes of limited transposition, was definitely established during his later years at the Paris Conservatory. His first published compositions, *Le banquet céleste* for organ (1928) and *Préludes pour piano* (1929) were written, using this original chromatic harmony.

The set of *Préludes* is important because it reflects his early individuality as well as the indications of his future maturity. The work contains the basic harmonic fundamentals of his craft, including the modes and added notes such as the added sixth and augmented fourth. The *Préludes* illustrate Messiaen's use of the modal harmonies with a tonal center and formal construction. Devices such as the thematic canon, already appearing in this work, foreshadow later developments.

Messiaen's *Préludes* have been compared in stature with the suite *Pour le piano* by Claude Debussy. Although Messiaen was inspired and influenced by the older composer in his early years, the *Préludes* cannot be considered derivative. Both works are poetic, however, in the sense that they reflect coloristic images inspired by their titles. The title of each prelude was designed in the style of Debussy's composition. Here their art differs. With the exception of mode 1 (the whole-tone scale), which Debussy used extensively, Messiaen's use of modal harmony was unique. The modes, being limited, produce a static effect. Debussy's music has this static quality as well, not because he used the same modes, but because of his own style. The formal processes of both composers, although comparable, were also not the same. Each wrote many of his works in short forms, yet while the music of both reflects the poetic thought suggested by the titles, Debussy's music is continually evolving of itself without meeting the demands of a fixed form. Messiaen, in the *Préludes,* used a variety of traditional forms such as the sonata, binary, or rondo form.

Prélude No. 2, "Chant d'extase dans un paysage triste," describes a "Song of Ecstasy from a Mournful Landscape." The mood of the composition is consistent with the title, in that the principal and subordinate theme express the two main stated ideas. The first theme conveys the feeling of a "mournful landscape" from which we could be hearing a "chant of ecstasy" in the mood of the second theme. The last section of the piece brings the return of the first theme. Constructed as a rondo, each section of the *ABA* form is a ternary form in itself: *abacdcaba.*

Outline of ternary form in *Prélude No. 2*

Section *A*   song sentence (measures 1–24)

a—first period, theme	(measures 1–11)
b—middle period	(measures 12–16)
a'—final period; varied reprise	(measures 17–24)

Section *B*   (measures 25–48)

c,c'—first period, theme	(measures 25–32)
d—middle period	(measures 33–40)
c,c'—exact reprise of theme	(measures 41–48)

Section *A'*   (measures 49–74)

a'—final period of section *A*	(measures 49–59)
b—middle period	(measures 60–64)
a—original theme	(measures 65–74)

Example 7. *Prélude No. 2,* section *A,* measures 1–11

The rhythmic notation of this piece illustrates his second category of notation in which he uses traditional notation and barlines to indicate the meter. Messiaen establishes here the practice of carefully marking all dynamics, accents, tempo, and phrasing choices. He never leaves these to chance or to the performer.

The opening theme of section *A* contains two distinct features of his melodic technique: the tritone, ascending to start the theme and then descending for a melodic cadence; and thematic development by means of recurring chromatic formulas, a pattern or motif based on a series of chromatic half-steps. Example 7 illustrates the opening theme with an incomplete cadence at measure 11. The fragments marked x are tritone intervals in the opening theme; fragments y, the chromatic formulas.

The tonality of the first section is F-sharp minor, mixed with tones of the three transpositions of mode 2. Measures 1 through 8 consist entirely of the tones belonging to mode 2, first transposition. Messiaen often includes tones from other transpositions of the same mode, which he calls "borrowing from itself."[1] Here mode 2 borrows from itself by including tones from the same mode, second transposition (measures 9 through 11), and then again same mode, third transposition (measures 12 through 14). Measure 9 is essentially in the first transposition of mode 2, with the exception of F and B, which belong to the second transposition. These two tones, however, present the tritone interval one-half step lower. The cadence in measure 11 emphasizes C-sharp which is anticipated briefly beginning in measure 9. Moving from F-sharp to C-sharp is a tonic-to-dominant relationship.

The middle section, beginning at measure 12, is in C minor. It is structurally significant that the tritone in the first theme, F-sharp to B-sharp, now appears in the tonal relationship of the first two periods, F-sharp to C. Motif fragments of chromatic formula y become thematic material for development in the middle period (measures 12 through 16). For example, the top line, first four notes, bar 14, repeats the chromatic intervals of y, bar 3, starting on a different tone.

Harmonically, the passage is of interest. Through the use of tones borrowed from transpositions of itself (mode 2), the music moves from C minor to C-sharp minor (measure 14) to C-sharp major (measure 16), the dominant of the original tonality F-sharp minor. While emphasizing the tone of C, Messiaen continues to reiterate F-sharp (see middle line, measures 12 and 15 in the score). This illustrates what Messiaen has termed an "atmosphere of several tonalities at once, without polytonality, the composer being free to give predominance to one of the tonalities or to leave the tonal impression unsettled."[2] Mode 2 in its first transposition "can hesitate between the four major tonalities of C, E-flat, F-sharp, and A."[3] By the frequent return of the tonic of the chosen key or by the use of the dominant seventh chord in that key, the mode mixes with the major tonality. In measure 16, the dominant seventh prepares for the varied repeat of the first theme, beginning in measure 17.

The reprise (measures 17 through 24) varies the theme by octave transpositions and doubling of melody and accompaniment. Additional variation occurs by adding the reverse order of the whole-step tone pattern in the bass and treble clefs of measures 17 and 18. The beginning chord of the final period, with these added notes, becomes the F-sharp minor chord with added sixth, another of Messiaen's favorite chords. A cadence on the tonic triad F-sharp minor completes the first section.

The second section of "Chant d'extase" provides a complete contrast to the first. The tempo increases, a change to the key of F-sharp major brightens the tonality; a new theme appears, again constructed on the

Example 8. *Prélude No. 2,* section *B,* measures 25–28

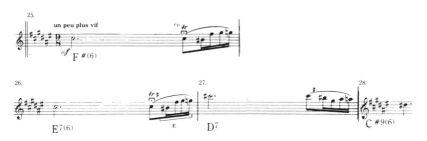

tritone (augment fourth and diminished fifth) and the chromatic formula (see Example 8). It is significant that Messiaen now uses the chromatic formula fragment as a group of passing tones foreign to the basic harmony. Example 8 illustrates this formula in the harmonic context. Messiaen cites the bracketed E fragment as constituting a "passing group" in this instance.[4] This progression is a "symmetrical movement, ascending or descending, degree by degree, of passing notes."[5]

The thematic line of this middle section (see Example 8, also middle line of Example 9) is still in mode 2, first transposition, where the predominant tone is again C-sharp, the dominant tone of F-sharp major. An added tone for color, borrowed from the second transposition, is G-sharp, the dominant tone of C-sharp.

Another characteristic feature of Messiaen's technique, a ninth chord with added sixth, is evident at measure 28. Here this C-sharp^9 chord introduces a series of ascending seventh chords, which leads to a repetition of the theme, this time with a melodic descent. Messiaen has indicated by a plus sign (+) the added notes to given chords. The basic chords to which notes have been added in measure 28 are the C-sharp^9, a diminished seventh, F-sharp^7, and A^7 chords (see Example 9).

In section *B,* the second theme or middle period *(d)* provides an excellent example containing several techniques characteristic of Messiaen's style: (1) two-part canon; (2) rhythmic pedal; and (3) non-retrogradable rhythm pattern ♪♩♪ . The canon in outside voices at a distance of a dotted quarter note begins at measure 33 and continues for three bars (see Example 10; J indicates rhythmic pedal with non-retrogradable pattern; K indicates two-part canon).

Example 9. *Prélude No. 2,* section *B,* measure 28

Example 10. *Prélude No. 2,* section *B,* measures 33–35

At measure 36 a cascade of chords interrupts the canon and outlines the
tritone in a descending sequence. These chords are modulatory, leading to
a repetition of the canon a whole tone higher. The two-part canon with
rhythmic pedal in the inner voice repeats in measures 37 through 40 to lead
to the return of the first theme at measure 41.

Measures 41 through 48 offer an exact repetition of theme *c,* progress-
ing into the varied recapitulation of section *A.*

Section *A* occurs in reverse order with *a', b, a.* This completes an
overall formal structure similar to the concept of Messiaen's non-
retrogradable rhythms in the sense that there is a central point (middle

section) dividing two groups, one of which is the retrograde of the other. The rondo is symmetrical in form.

Measure 73 repeats the tritone theme of the first four notes in harmony, shortening the theme successively in measure 74. The melodic motif is next reduced to two notes, the initial tritone fragment. The final chord, the F-sharp major tonic triad with added sixth, decreased to *ppppp*, concludes the piece.

Important characteristic features that are part of Messiaen's early stylistic development include chromatic formulas and the tritone interval that he favored in melodic construction. Messiaen's use of the second mode of limited transposition mixed with the basic tonality, his added notes to traditional seventh chords, and his use of foreign notes such as the passing group illustrate ingredients of the early harmonic practice of his craft. His use of two-part canon, rhythmic pedal, and non-retrogradable rhythm indicate that many fundamentals of Messiaen's art were already present. Although he later developed these devices with imagination and added others, he used them most effectively in this work.

4

Thème and Variations (1932)

Messiaen's love of colors began when he was a child, in the contemplation of nature around him and from viewing stained-glass windows. When his father was named a professor in Paris, Messiaen had opportunity to visit monuments, churches, and museums. He found the marvelous colors in the windows of Notre Dame, Sainte Chapelle, and the cathedral of Chartres fascinating. He considers these manmade creations to be manifestations of nature: the construction of nature's light in all its glorious varieties.

Messiaen believes sound to be inextricably bound to color, that the correspondence of sound and color rests in scientific truth, which is then colored by the personality of the one who is gifted with synesthesia. Messiaen's friend, Swiss painter Charles Blanc-Gatti, had an irregularity of his optical and auditory nerves that permitted him to see colors and forms when he listened to music. Messiaen has stated that he sees spiritually the corresponding colors when he hears a score or when he reads a score (listening mentally). About 1931 Blanc-Gatti and Messiaen performed an experiment that established a distinct correlation between specific colors and sounds. Messiaen performed one of his own compositions and Blanc-Gatti painted the colors the sounds produced in his mind's eye. Messiaen confirmed that the colors were identical to those conceived spiritually during actual composition of the music.

Since the majority of people do not have the ability to visualize colors with sound, we can only try to imagine what Messiaen sees as he interchanges his modes. Artists in all media should be able to relate to the composer's use of whatever inspires creative responses from within.

Messiaen has never drawn inspiration for his musical writing by contemplating colors on a canvas. On the contrary, he visualizes and then uses

39

the colors that are caused by the sonorities he has created. In structuring his composition then, he arranges complementary colors as a painter would do in a painting, emphasizing and blending as his composition unfolds. His approach to form in the early years was to a large extent dictated by this sound-color approach.

The *Thème and Variations* for violin and piano was composed in 1932. Messiaen was still very involved with the modes of limited transposition, but he had begun to seek means of developing his harmonies further by technical means other than the juxtaposition of colors. *Prélude No. 2* reflected his attitude to harmony as a static element, which is a direct result of his goal to suspend the sense of time in music. We have seen how his purpose to express the idea of the eternal as distinct from the temporal influenced his philosophy concerning rhythm. Because the regular pulse is inconceivable to Messiaen, time becomes an accumulation of moments in eternity. Upon a framework of this view of time and of nonprogressive harmony, Messiaen evolved the style and inner chromatic motion that is consistent with his purposes.

David Drew, in his discerning analytical discussion of Messiaen's techniques, has offered an explanation of the lack of harmonic progression:

The tonic is like a ring to which the harmony is attached. The modes are like an immensely long rope that allows it to rove across a wide field, whilst all the time imposing a certain constraint. (Obviously the modes allow a great variety of chromatic chords that may be clearly related to one tonal pole.) The composer is thus able to juxtapose chords that have only the remotest diatonic relationship to one another, with the result that whilst the music is externally in a state of what one might call tonal catalepsy, internally it is in constant motion. The situation is paradoxical; perhaps it is easier to understand if we regard the tonality as being at once ubiquitous and unchanging—a state of affairs that may be justifiably regarded as an allegory for the Divine Order.[1]

In the *Prélude No. 2* Messiaen expresses the cadential impluse mainly by certain melodic tones, while the chromatic harmonies remains fluid. The music, intimately connected with his philosophy, contains one center with an atmosphere created by the elaboration of that center. Although the early pieces were successful, the harmonic limitations raised questions. How would Messiaen compose larger works? How would he create variety in a larger form?

Theme and variations was one of the first means Messiaen used in approaching a larger composition. Regarding the work, Drew says,

This is not an ambitious work; still less is it a perfect one. But by and large, it is one of the most valuable of Messiaen's early compositions. It did not, however, indicate any permanent way of escape from the impasse into which Messiaen's anti-developmental aesthetic had led him.[2]

Thème and Variations uses the classical form to provide inventive changes of his melodic theme. It differs from the classical form in that his harmony does not follow a progressive pattern that would serve as the basis for each new variation. Was a crisis becoming apparent because the harmonic language could not create extended structures? It had obviously become necessary to explore new creative territory.

Thème and Variations is representative of Messiaen's compositional techniques developed thus far. It is conventional, with a theme in the first section and five subsequent variations. Messiaen constructed the theme in a very characteristic manner, the song sentence.

The song sentence consists of the (1) theme (antecedent and consequent); (2) middle period; and (3) final period, an issue of the theme. In Example 11, the theme is divided into *AA'BC*. The brackets indicate the theme (bars 1 through 7) divided into three sections: x, y, and x. Messiaen develops these fragments individually as the work progresses.

The middle period (bars 15 through 20) uses the intervals of fragment y in six versions from different degrees of the mode. Fragment y changes melodically and rhythmically; the tritone is evident in all its repetitions.

The final period *C* (bars 21 through 28) derives from the theme, using the thematic fragments of x and z for its concluding statement. Fragment x repeats twice on different degrees of the mode; z returns once to conclude the first section.

The piece begins in conventional 4/4 rhythmic notation. The main tone heard in the variations is F-sharp. In the first theme of the violin, the F-sharp moves down the modal scale of mode 3, first transposition (F-sharp, E, E-flat, D, to C), the first tone (F-sharp) forming a tritone relationship with the last tone (C). This work is modal throughout, belonging entirely to various transpositions of mode 3. The modal scheme of the theme is *A* and *A'*, melody and harmony belong to mode 3, first transposition. The melody and harmony of the final period *C* also belongs to mode 3, first transposition. The middle period *B* is a commentary on the theme, which according to Messiaen's definition is a

. . . melodic development of the theme, one in which some fragments of the theme are repeated in the initial key upon different degrees, or in other keys, and are varied rhythmically, melodically, and harmonically.[3]

Example 11. *Thème and Variations,* theme, measures 1–28

Extract from *Thème and Variations* by Oliver Messiaen. Copyright by Alphonse Leduc & Cie., Paris, France.

In *B* section the y fragments vary as they move to different degrees of the mode: the first, third, and sixth version of y belong to mode 3, first transposition, while y^2, y^4, and y^5 belong to mode 3, fourth transposition.

The harmonic structure of the theme, although it belongs to the same mode, contrasts in line and texture to the theme. While the left hand plays whole notes as a fixed melody, the right hand moves, ascending and descending, in thirds. (Messiaen's notation appears here as diminished fourths and augmented seconds.) At B the style changes completely, with three tones in a descending pattern harmonized by a series of alternate major and minor chords. The harmony does not correspond to the melodic y divisions modally, but follows its own pattern of shifting to various transpositions of mode 3. At C the left hand moves down the modal scale in whole notes of third mode, first transposition, ending on G. While the harmony sounds a C major 6/4 chord to close the theme, violin is playing A-*flat* the lowered sixth degree of C major, which adds to the suspension quality of the 6/4 chord and prepares the ear for the beginning of the next section.

First variation

The format of the first variation remains the same as the original theme, or $AA'BC$. The rhythm is still a conventional 4/4 notation, and the mode continues to be in first transposition of mode 3. This variation contains more motion with constant movement in eighth notes and triplets, right hand, contrasted with eighth and quarter notes, pianissimo in the left hand. The entire theme A (violin) is in the introduction this time (piano part, right hand), with passing tones added. The clever application of the intervallic third is a striking feature. The entire accompanying harmony of the original theme is in the piano, left hand. The violin enters once more at A', repeating the melody with the variation of chromatic passing tones in eighth notes and triplets.

Accompanying the melody at A' is what Messiaen calls a pedal group, defined as follows:

Instead of one sustained note, foreign to the chords which surround it, we shall have a repeated music (repetition and sustaining are equivalent), foreign to another music situated above or below it; each of these musics will have its own rhythm, melody, and harmonies.[4]

In example 12 the top line of the piano part becomes a pedal group, repeating the same harmonic and rhythmic pattern, irrespective of the melody and harmony around it, for seven bars. This pedal group is also modal, belonging to the third mode, first transposition.

Variation in B section, as well as in C, continues to follow the pattern of increasing the motion of fragments y (section B), and also x and z (section C), through the use of passing and neighboring tones. At B both hands of the accompaniment reinforce the violin melody. With this repetition of the same notes of the melody in the piano part, the texture becomes thicker.

Example 12. *Thème and Variations,* first variation, section *A'*, measures 35–40

Extract from *Thème and Variations* by Oliver Messiaen. Copyright by Alphonse Leduc & Cie., Paris, France.

At bar 45 the left hand of the piano plays the melodic fragment y in a two-bar interlude as the right hand carries the harmony of the original theme. In this application of the harmony, Messiaen alternates major and minor chords with a diminution of the original rhythmic pattern. This results in a Messiaenic version of double counterpoint, which occurs throughout the two-bar interlude. Notable also at bar 45 is the harmonic relationship to the melody. In the top and bottom lines of the harmony, the intervallic distance from the melody is consistently that of a half-step or a major second. This *B* section contains the same shifting of modal harmonies that are in the original theme, due to the repetition of the varied y fragment on different degrees of the mode.

At *C* (bar 49) the pedal group heard earlier in section *A'* returns, third mode, first transposition. This time the "repeated foreign music" continues for eight bars. The harmony occurs entirely in the left hand, with octave doublings and added ninth chords. Tones of the violin theme also reinforce the melody. This harmony appears in an eighth-note pattern that repeats itself in a quasi-mini-pedal group pattern. This "music" is not foreign to the theme, however; it is the original harmony of the theme.

Moving down the notes of the modal scale, third mode, first transposition, the harmony arrives in measure 55 to the C6/4 chord with lowered sixth degree that closed the theme. Messiaen emphasizes this tone in repetition throughout bars 55 and 56. In this first variation, however, the *A-flat* progresses stepwise down to *F,* in the final bar.

The violin plays an embellishing line of the z fragment with a sudden drop to an E-sharp (F) to conclude this section. This is the only tone that is foreign to the third mode, first transposition; it acts as a suspension tone, moving up to the F-sharp of the final chord. At the resolution point in the last bar, the two borrowed or nonmodal tones (D-sharp suspension and C-sharp, which formed part of the major triad, same measure) now move to their neighboring tones (F-sharp and C), which completes the variation in mode 3, first transposition. Variation One, in its conclusion, however, leaves the listener with a sense of suspended motion, and an expectancy of more to come.

Second Variation

The format of Variation Two is A (introduction) $A'BCA^2BA^3A^4$ and coda. Variation Two shifts to compound time with a staccato rendition, in 12/8 meter, of the entire A theme in diminution as in bars 59 and 60 (see Example 13).

Example 13. *Thème and Variations*, second variation, section A, measures 59–60

In the next two bars, A' repeats the theme a tritone above the original; this is achieved by using the third transposition of mode 3 rather than the first.

In Variation Two Messiaen uses two important techniques of the fugue form (episode and stretto), which he considers to be its essential parts. In contradiction to our usual concept, Messiaen defines episode as a "progression of harmony, concealed by entrances in canonic imitation being reproduced at symmetrical intervals, generally from fifth to fifth."[6] Although the piece avoids harmonic progressions, in section B at measures 65 and 66 (where the episode occurs), the harmony moves in a cycle of fifths from G to C, F to B-flat, and finally to E-flat where C section begins.

Example 14. *Thème and Variations,* second variation, section *B,* measures 65–66

Extract from *Thème and Variations* by Olivier Messiaen. Copyright by Alphonse Leduc & Cie., Paris, France.

In Example 14 the bracketed material in the piano part indicates the material of theme *A* transposed up one degree; this material is repeated at symmetrical intervals in canonic imitation. The entrance of each imitative voice occurs at intervals a fifth apart (encircled in Example 14). In bars 65 and 66, Messiaen has inverted the material of measures 59 and 60, a compositional technique that defines double counterpoint. The melodic materials heard in the first measure of Variation Two, piano part, upper and lower staves have been inverted; the melodic fragment of the piano part, lower stave, has moved to the violin part. This passage necessitates the use of nearly all transpositions of mode 3.

At *C* Messiaen uses only the x fragment of original theme. Developing sequentially, it moves up one-half step, a minor third, and another one-half step. The harmony in this passage alternates between the first and fourth transpositions of mode 3. Fragment x changes again in bar 69 by means of the compositional technique of elimination. The first three notes remain, to repeat successively on higher degrees of mode 3, third transposition (bars 69 and 70) until the sequential movement arrives at the return point of theme *A* (bar 71).

Messiaen credits Beethoven with creating melodic development through elimination. Citing the first movement of *Symphony No. 5 in C Minor,* he places this procedure at the basis of all thematic life. The technique is simply one of "repeating a fragment of the theme, taking away from it successively a part of its notes up to concentration upon itself, reduction to a schematic state, shrunken by strife, by crisis."[7]

Section *C* also illustrates the use of two transpositions of a mode simultaneously; mode 3, third transposition appears in the violin part (bars 69 and 70), while the piano harmony is in mode 3, first transposition.

At *A²* the melodic variation on the original theme occurs in the violin part (bar 71), this time one octave higher. Brackets in measure 71 of

Example 15. *Thème and Variations,* second variation, section A^2, measures 71–72

Extract from *Thème and Variations* by Olivier Messiaen. Copyright by Alhponse Leduc & Cie., Paris, France.

Example 15 indicate Messiaen's use of stretto in triple canon at the octave. The stretto appears at one eighth note's distance in each voice. The middle voice of this canon (bar 71) contains parallel major and minor triads with the melodic line on top. All voices blend in the modal harmony of third mode, third transposition (bars 72 and 73); this harmony follows a sequential pattern using fragment y of theme A in its descent and arrival at section B.

Section B, the connective material, consists of fragments y and x of the original theme. Both fragments appear only once; in its transitional function, B hints at thematic repetition before returning to the original theme of the beginning of Variation Two.

Theme A^3 repeats the original thematic fragment (x and y) and varies it immediately by repeating it one-half step below the original. The same sequential descent that occurred at A^2 appears here, using reduced fragment y in third mode, third transposition, which moves through to A^4 (bar 77).

Section A_4 reiterates the original theme of this work in a more exact form, differing only slightly in rhythmic pattern. Although Messiaen uses only fragments x and y, he dispenses with the technique of diminution in this section. At bar 79, y repeats in a truncated sequential pattern, alternating modal transpositions. A short coda begins at bar 81, consisting of the thematic A in diminution. The coda restates the y fragment of original theme through four octaves, and ends this variation on a suspension note of the B natural, with all voices in third mode, first transposition.

Third Variation

Variation Three continues with the original thematic material x and y. In this variation one finds many metric changes; nearly each measure has a different meter signature. Messiaen has written Variation Three in second notation. The barlines designate meter changes and accent.

The form of Variation Three is a repeated parallel period separated by a transition.

Section *A*	(bars 85–90)
Section *A'*	(bars 91–97)
Transition	(bars 98–101)
Section *A²*	(bars 102–106)
Section *A³*	(bars 107–115)

Messiaen has written Variation Three entirely in mode 3, first transposition, and mode 3, fourth transposition except for the transitional section. In varying the theme he uses the chromatic formulas that he favored in early works, including the *Préludes*. The harmony consists mainly of major triads in root position in the right hand, using a contrary motion in both hands, and offering a polychordal effect.

In section *A'* contrary motion of the harmony continues (measure 92), and the same relationship between the hands is evident; the major triads of the right hand move up in a whole-step intervallic pattern; major triads in the left hand descend in a one-half–step pattern (see Example 16).

Example 16. *Thème and Variations,* third variation, section *A'*, measures 91–93

Extract from *Thème and Variations* by Olivier Messiaen. Copyright by Alphonse Leduc & Cie., Paris, France.

At measure 93 a fortissimo chord combines two diminished seventh chords (C-sharp E G A-sharp and D E-sharp G-Sharp B). This chord resolves to an augmented chord with a dissonant D in the bass. A repetition of these chords occurs in measure 94.

After a modulatory transitional section, the melodic and harmonic material reappears transposed one-half step up from the original period of the variation in the violin part. The transitional phrase (bars 98 through 101) consists of a motive in sequence moving up to the new transposition of mode 3, while descending chords in fourths form the accompaniment.

Variation Three continues to center around the tone of F-sharp. Significant is the one tone, C-sharp (the dominant of F-sharp), which occurs frequently and does not belong to the first transposition of mode 3.

Fourth Variation

Variation Four returns to simple 4/4 meter with the same rhythm throughout. This variation is primarily in third mode, first transposition, with the exception of modulatory passages, which use the second and third transpositions of the same mode.

The format of this variation is *ABA'B'C* and coda, while the basic melodic design consists of connecting notes from fragments x and y. One can see the derivation from the original theme, but the result cannot easily be recognized.

The rhythm in the piano part adds excitement by the use of triplets in the left hand against eighth notes in the right hand. At *B'* the triplet pattern continues, now using both staves of the piano.

Each previous variation has built up momentum, gradually leading to this climactic point of the entire work. The rhythm adds to the momentum as it moves from the relatively simple presentations of theme in quarter notes, to eighth notes in the third, and the tempo change in the fourth variation. Dynamic markings for the violin and piano are *vif* and *passionne* (with "fire" and "passion"). The harmony of this variation still uses the original harmony of the theme in third mode, first transposition. Triplets in the piano part that consist of broken triads in second inversion and perfect and diminished fourths from the mode help to increase tension.

At section *B* a suggestion of fragments y and z occur in the violin (measures 124 through 127). The piano, left hand of *B* section has downward chromatic motion for four measures as the passage returns to *A* with renewed force. After an exact repetition of *A* this chromatic movement begins again at *B'*, this time a major third higher (measure 134). Also, *B'* is more intensified at this point, starting the y movement from higher peaks, reiterating this fragment from various degrees, then reversing the order of the intervals. The violin repeats the y fragment in downward, unwinding motion, coinciding with the chromatic line of the left hand, which continues through two octaves (measures 134 through 141). Harmonies within the modal context include major thirds combined with major seconds (see measure 135 in score), major seconds with minor thirds (measure 136), and diminished triads (measure 136).

The material in section C continues the descent, which, except for brief crescendos, diminishes in intensity. Messiaen continues the unifying influence of the third (tenths) in the outer voices. Thematic content in this section consists of connective fragments of x and y (measures 142 and 143), which repeat one whole step lower every two measures. At each repetition the rhythm remains constant as the intervallic movement changes.

A long coda concludes this variation, beginning an upward chromatic movement at measure 149. While the left hand plays a pedal on F-sharp, the inner voice of the right hand moves up the modal scale of third mode, first transposition (measure 150).

The chromatic motion continues to rise for three measures, returns to its starting point, and builds again. This motif repeats three times, until at measure 162 the rising line has reached the final trill on E. The suspension quality continues through the last beat of the final measure when the E moves up chromatically, not reaching the recurring F-sharp until the beginning of Variation Five.

Fifth Variation

Variation Five has, for the first time, a different harmonization of the melodic theme. This harmonization accompanies the violin theme, which has returned to the original theme, although one octave higher. Directed to be played *ffff*, this variation completes the climactic intensity. It now begins the descent in intensity, subsiding gradually to the end of the variation. The format is like the original $AA'BC$, with a brief coda at the end.

At A' the accompaniment repeats the modal harmony of the original, with octave doublings of each voice thickening the texture. At the end of section A (measures 179 and 180), the melody moves up one-half step, causing a brief shift to the fourth transposition of mode 3. The harmony, belonging to fourth transposition here also, has added seventh chords that begin pianissimo, and crescendo once more to *ffff* (section B).

At B the harmony contains harmonies of mode 3 as well as major triads, minor triads, and seventh chords. In the last two measures of section B (185 and 186), the major and minor triads alternate in a descending pattern.

Section C (measures 187 through 194) begins with fragment x and concludes with the z fragment heard in measures 191 and 192 and again in measures 193 and 194. This fragment, which had concluded the original theme, occurred infrequently during the intervening variations. The statement of this concluding phrase then moves into a coda beginning at measure 195, with a stepwise descending chromatic movement. A pedal point on B natural extends throughout eight measures of the ten-measure coda in the left hand of the piano. In the violin part, the y fragment briefly interrupts the stepwise motion at measure 200 before the conclusion of the piece, triple pianissimo, measure 204.

Many of the compositional techniques that Messiaen has used in *Thème and Variations* follow traditional lines of theory and indicate the soundness of his academic training. He uses devices to develop his thematic material, such as melodic elimination and diminution of rhythm, which have been present in comsitions since the late Baroque period. Messiaen's use of the song sentence for his theme and his employment of the traditional variation form reveal his ability to write imaginative music that has shape and structure. His desire to depart from the expected theoretical progressions led him to combine his modal harmonies within this traditional structure and to find new means of providing continuity, of building tension and momentum. Polyphonic devices such as canonic imitation, stretto, episode, and double counterpoint further enhance the credibility of his music. The pedal group appearing in this work foreshadows Messiaen's extensive use of this feature in later compositions. The work reflects vividly the combination of tradition with new discovery that is apparent in compositions of his early years.

5

La nativité du Seigneur (1935)

Messiaen completed his studies at the Paris Conservatory in 1930. In 1931, at the age of twenty-two he was appointed organist of the church of la Sainte Trinité, Paris. He has held this important position throughout his life since those early days, when he was acclaimed as the best young organist in France.

Many of the parishoners of la Trinité were older, conservative patrons who preferred traditional church music. With Messiaen as organist, they were introduced to a new sound produced by the improvisations he was exploring constantly. To some people, Messiaen's improvisations called to mind the voice of the devil; they complained loudly, demanding the conventional music they were used to. To Messiaen this music was sickly sweet and rather boring. Throughout this conflict, the clergy was supportive, understanding that Messiaen's improvisations were based on his own interpretations of the Scriptures.

Eventually a schedule was worked out that satisfied both Messiaen and the congregation: On Sunday during High Mass he played only plainchant; at eleven o'clock Low Mass he played classical and romantic music; at noon Mass Messiaen's own works could be heard; at five o'clock Vespers service he was allowed to improvise. Now the people knew what to expect during different services and gradually there were those who came specifically to hear Messiaen's works and improvisations. Just as Dupré and Tournemire, organ masters who preceded his generation, Messiaen was beginning to inspire his own following.

He always built his improvisations with a sense of form and order, in keeping with the traditional schooling he had received at the Conservatory. Many were in styles other than his own; he could imitate with facility Mozart, Bach, Schumann, and Debussy. Only a few years later, in fact, he

53

wrote a book of lessons in harmony that were created in the styles of major composers from Monteverdi to Ravel.

In 1934, only two years after his own graduation from school, Messiaen began to teach chamber music and sight reading at the Ecole Normale de Musique. Two years later he taught a course in organ improvisation at the Schola Cantorum. So the pattern of his life was fairly well established by his early twenties: he had an important position as organist in Paris; he had begun to establish himself as a teacher; and he was composing his first major work with the confidence that belongs to those with great talent and promise.

La nativité du Seigneur, Messiaen's first major work, was written at Grenoble in 1934 and first performed at Trinity Church the same year. The first of a number of lengthy works, it lasts one hour and consists of four books containing nine movements. Messiaen has indicated in *Technique* that he considers it to be characteristic of his musical language. He has preceded each movement by a quotation from Scriptures that relates to the work's theological meaning.

This aspect of the work contains five fundamental principles[1]: (1) our predestination realized in the Incarnation of the Word; (2) God living in the midst of us, God suffering; (3) the three incarnations—the Eternal Word, the Temporal Christ, and Christian Spirituality; (4) the characters giving the celebration its own particular poetry; and (5) nine movements in all to honor the maternity of the Blessed Virgin.

The first piece, "La Vierge et l'Enfant," describes the joy of the Virgin Mary at the birth of the child Christ: "Conceived by a Virgin a Child is born to us, unto us a Son is given. Rejoice greatly, O daughter of Zion! Behold thy King cometh unto thee, he is just and humble."[2]

In *La nativité* the development of Messiaen's ametrical rhythmic style is apparent. In subsequent works it becomes evident that his rhythmic innovations are a highly significant factor in the creation of larger forms for his music. Here he introduced the added value, which caused an effect of stretching or contracting the time values in a passage that would otherwise be basically metrical. The added value also facilitated the writing of Greek meter, which Messiaen began to use at this time. It is also directly related to the Hindu rhythms that were appearing in Messiaen's music during the period of rhythmic development that followed the composition of *La nativité.*

"La Vierge et l'Enfant" is in the form of a traditional rondo. The first *A* may be divided *aa*[1]*bb*[1]. Messiaen has based the *B* section theme on a plainchant tune from the Introit for the third Mass of Christmas: *Puer natus est nobis*[3] ("A child is born for us, a Son is given to us; whose kingdom is upon his shoulder, and his name shall be the Angel of great council").

Outline of ternary form in *La nativité du Seigneur*

Section *A*   (measures 1–15)

> *a, a′* —theme, first period   (measures 1–7)
> *a, b′* —variation on theme, second period
>   (measures 3–15)

Section *B*   (measures 16–34)

> *c* —theme   (measures 16–23)
> *c′* —theme, new vertical alignment   (measures 23–34)

Section *A*   (measures 35–45)

> a^2 —original theme, transposed   (measures 35–38)
> a^3 —original theme with embellishment at cadence
>   (measures 39–45)

The melodic theme of section *A* is similar to the opening five notes of Moussorgsky's *Boris Godounov*. Messiaen derives his own "cadential formula"[4] from this theme, which uses the favored descending augmented fourth (see Example 17).

Example 17. *La nativité due Seigneur*, "La Vierge et l'Enfant," measure 1

Extract from *La nativité du Seigneur* by Olivier Messiaen. Copyright by Alphonse Leduc & Cie., Paris, France.

The entire first period *(aa′)* is in the second mode, first transposition; thus Messiaen has transformed *Godounov's* motif to conform to his own modal system. In this case the predominant color of the music would be "crimson-blue violet" according to Messiaen's definitions.[5]

In measure one of "La Vierge" (Example 17), the added value is indicated by a + (plus) sign. The addition of the sixteenth note produces ametrical music in a piece that would otherwise be basically metrical, with regular 3/4 time division at the beginning. Use of the added value thus produces the asymmetrical grouping of thirteen sixteenth-note values, being compatible with Messiaen's basic philosophy concerning rhythm.

This added value became instrumental in the notating of Greek rhythms that he began to use. In the first measure of "La Vierge," bracketed notes in Example 17 indicate the antibacchic peon (𝅘𝅥𝅮𝅘𝅥𝅮 𝅘𝅥𝅮), a Greek time division.

In the second period of the first section *A* Messiaen broadens the spectrum of tonal colors by modulation from one mode to another. In example 18, within the span of three measures, one can note the movement from one mode to another. The first measure is in third mode, first

Example 18. *La nativité du Seigneur,* "La Vierge et l'Enfant," measures 8–10

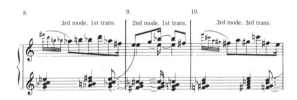

Extract from *La nativité du Seigneur* by Olivier Messiaen. Copyright by Alphonse Leduc & Cie., Paris, France.

transposition; it moves in the second measure to second mode, first transposition; while the third measure contains the notes of third mode, third transposition. This example illustrates the ability of the modes to modulate freely to themselves or to other modes, mingling the tonal colors that Messiaen has at his disposal. He often used various modes and their transpositions to depict emotions he wished to convey in the theological portrait, which is always specifically titled and defined in his notes.

Messiaen bases the entire section *B* on the repetition and variation of three elements found entirely in the first two measures (see Example 19).

The top line, or melody, drawn from *Puer natus est nobis* plainchant theme varies consistently throughout the section. In the left hand are eleven chords per measure, which form a harmonic pedal, or ostinato, that repeats throughout the section. The only alteration of these chords appears at a cadential point. In the pedal line there is a musical line built on the notes d, f, e, g-sharp, and d, which is the *Godounov* melodic pattern. The rhythmic pattern of this pedal carillon is 3 + 3 + 5, which corresponds to the eleven chords per measure of the left hand. As the *B* section pro-

La nativité du Seigneur (1935) 57

Example 19. *La nativité du Seigneur,* "La Vierge," *B* section, measures 16–17

Extract from *La nativité du Seigneur* by Olivier Messiaen. Copyright by Alphonse Leduc & Cie., Paris, France.

gresses, the pitches of the carillon vary in order, as do the small time values within the 6 + 5 relationship. These changes indicate Messiaen's early use of melodic and rhythmic permutation that he developed in future compositions. In the entire section *B,* all three musical lines belong to mode 6, first transposition. Therefore one finds that the original plainchant theme, redesigned to fit the sixth mode, joined with the rhythmic variations of a pedal carillon of shrill timbre, and blended with the harmonic pedal of eleven chords, also in sixth mode, has transformed into the style Messiaen.

Most significant in this music is the dissociation of rhythm and harmony. The harmonic pedal of eleven units is similar to a Hindu tâla and becomes the fundamental pattern against which other rhythms contrast. The rhythmic working provides tension and relaxation, cadential effects no longer found in the harmony. At this point it is notable that time signatures no longer occur in Messiaen's music.

In the variation of *c,* bar 23, the upper melody begins one measure sooner, causing a completely new vertical alignment. Although the ingredients of the music remain the same for a complete repetition of *c* in section *B,* the resultant music is new. Melodic construction in the upper voice also changes in the second half of section *B,* and the subsection is extended for three measures. The pedal rhythm adds three new interpretations of an eighth-note meter throughout the extension at the end of *c'.* In the last interpretation, the pedal finally coincides rhythmically with the even eighth notes of the harmonic ostinato played by the left hand.

As these compositional techniques evolve with subsequent works, Messiaen's polyrhythms often result from the use of ostinato techniques. Once rhythm becomes dissociated from harmony, however, it is logical and easy to establish a rhythmic ostinato that is attached to, but independent of, another harmonic ostinato.

The final section (measures 35 through 45) repeats the original theme, now transposed to second mode, second transposition. The piece remains in this mode until the end, reaching a final cadence at measure 42. The final note D sustains for four bars, although interrupted by a single group of fifty-six notes. Messiaen describes this technique as an embellishment group[6] (see Example 20).

In regard to timbre, Messiaen continued the development of new approaches to the standard treatment of the French organ during this period. He produced unusual timbres by opposing rather than mixing the colors: the Gambe and Voix Celeste, opposed Flute 4', Nazard, Tierce, Piccolo 1'. At the same time the pedal Flute 4' added a shrill carillon effect that is on the same pitch register as the harmonic ostinato. The pedal's departure from its bass role and the use of a combination of manual stops that exclude the 8' pitch are notable innovations Messiaen made for the organ with this work.

In *La nativité* Messiaen shows a continuing evolution in his creative development and he also presents some new beginnings. In his melodies he continues to use cadential formulas and the augmented fourth interval as well as his original modes. The use of plainchant as a basis for melody begins with "La Vierge," middle section. Messiaen continues to explore the modes and to find new variety in their harmonies, adding chords that have a more dissonant effect. Important innovations that appear in *La nativité* are the added value, the introduction of Greek rhythmic patterns, early use of the rearrangement of rhythmic order, and the dissociation of rhythm and harmony. These are part of a continuing maturation in Messiaen's creative process rather than isolated ideas selected for special effects. With the vocal and piano works that follow, he further develops these techniques.

Example 20. *La nativité du Seigneur,* "La Vierge," embellishment group on D

Extract from *La nativité du Seigneur* by Olivier Messiaen. Copyright by Alphonse Leduc & Cie., Paris, France.

6

Poèmes Pour Mi (1936)

The group *La Jeune France,* which Messiaen had helped to organize for the purpose of restoring expression in music, began to receive a certain amount of recognition around this time. Helpful to their cause was the fact that they were recipients of some financial backing; however, they were soon to discover differences among themselves concerning which paths to pursue in order to achieve their mutual ideals. Yves Baudrier and Daniel Lesur wished to ignore questions of technique and musical language so as to give expression their prime consideration. The other two members, Messiaen and André Jolivet, were of the opinion that new techniques must be explored together with the search for deeper expression. Messiaen and Jolivet's philosophical position was particularly difficult to maintain because of the transitional period for music in which they were living. While they were opposing current composers whose main concern was technique, they themselves were searching for new techniques. Furthermore, their concern for expression was definitely a point of view counter to the current neoclassicism.

The brief life of *La Jeune France* came to an end during the disruptive period that accompanied the war. Each of the composers eventually felt it necessary to develop according to his own philosophical propensities.

The year 1936 was an important one for Messiaen; he married the violinist Claire Delbos, to whom he dedicated his first major song cycle, *Poèmes pour Mi,* written during that same year. "Mi" does not refer to the third scale-tone; it was a nickname Messiaen had for his wife. One year after their marriage, the couple had a son whom they named Pascal. Pascal was inspiration for the babe of whom Messiaen wrote in another major song cycle, *Chants de terre et de ciel* (1938).

Poèmes pour Mi relates to the sacramental and spiritual aspects of marriage, while *Chants de terre* is concerned with the themes of parenthood and childhood innocence. Although many of the personal events of Messiaen's life have been carefully concealed from public eye, some facts can be deduced from examining his music during this early period in his marriage. The poetry in *Poèmes pour Mi* would seem to indicate in certain movements that, even in the early stages, his first marriage was not entirely ideal. Within a few more years, tragedy touched the family. Claire Delbos contracted an incurable disease that slowly caused her complete deterioration. Eventually she was confined to a mental hospital where she gradually lost sight, motion, hearing, and reason. She died in 1959. This tragic turn of fate took a tremendous toll in anxiety and stress during many years of Messiaen's creative life.

Pascal has rarely been discussed by his father, who seemed determined to allow the boy to have a private life and pursue his own destiny. Pascal proceeded to follow the literary direction of his grandparents rather than music. At the present time he is a teacher of Russian in Paris; he has also written some poetry.

Poèmes pour Mi is divided into two books; the cycle consists of nine melodies (the number nine being a symbol of maternity), four in the first book, five in the second. "Le collier" ("The Necklace") is the eighth piece. The style of the songs varies considerably. Some are simple poetic impressions, evoking colors or perfume or the time of day, such as the selections "Paysage" or "Ta voix." There are theatrical scenes such as "Epouvante." Psalmodies and halleliuatic vocalises, such as those found in plainchant of the Middle Ages appear in the first selection, "Action de graces" and the ninth, "Prière exaucée."

"Le collier" is one of the more melodic texts in this cycle, foreshadowing the highly lyrical style of later works. The musical language is one of modal colors, often forming polymodality[1]; it is a continuation of the style espoused by Messiaen between 1929 and 1946.

It is significant that Messiaen has always written his own lyrics for his vocal works, texts that are integral to the composer's thought. Many critics have denigrated his poems; those who admire his music often overlook them. As the lyrics are conceived simultaneously with the music, it is really not appropriate to criticize them as a separate art form, as each would be less effective without the other. The songs of the first book relate to the preparation for marriage. The influence of French Symbolist poets is evident here; for example, symbols of nature such as the calm beauty of a lake contrasting with a road full of pitfalls might suggest the contrast between the security of married love and the problems of life.

The second book empahsizes the fulfillment of marriage; it begins with "L'epouse" (The Spouse). It describes the married state as a vocation and provides the link between single and married life. Symbolized here also in the subsequent songs is the fulfillment of marriage and the strength derived from this sacrament. Unity of marriage is expressed in the seventh song, "Je suis tes deux enfants, mon Dieu!" ("I am your two children, O my God!").

"Le collier" is also symbolic in terms of nature. It represents acceptance of the simple joy of union, of peace. The lyric begins:

Springtime captive,
lingering rainbow of the morning,
Ah, my yoke! Ah my necklace!
Oh, my little, lively support
for my wearied ears!

Necklace of springtime, of delight
and of grace,
Eastern necklace, rare necklace,
Multicolored as pearls and rosettes.
Curved countryside, landscape
Married to the fresh morning air.

Ah, my necklace! My necklace!
Your two arms entwined about
my neck this morning.

In the second compositional period, Messiaen began new rhythmic procedures that are evident in *Poèmes pour Mi,* but in rather undefined form. In "Le collier," rhythmic patterns use Indian decî-tâla, Greek meters, and non-retrogradable rhythms; however, the overall rhythmic design is unsystematic. The development of these innovative practices continued through the experimental period of 1949–1951.

Messiaen composed the poems and the music together, as he has done for all of his song cycles. Both his choice of rhythm and the melody line follow the speaking inflections of the poetry. Although written for a soprano, he expresses the soul of the man in his lyrics. Messiaen has written this work without time signature, using exact values and irregular measures and beat. It is a ternary sentence that includes a brief coda.

Formal outline of *Poèmes pour Mi*

Section *A* (measures 1–13)

    a—theme, three phrases (measures 1–13)

Section *B*   (measures 14–26)

    b—commentary, employing fragments of original theme

                                    (measures 14–18)

    c—phrase   (measures 19–26)

Section *A'*   (measures 27–39)

    a'—theme, three phrases   (measures 27–39)

Coda   (measures 40–51)

At the beginning *A* section, the first lyric speaks of the "captive" as linked or enchained. The piano translates this poetic image into musical terms with a repetition on three chords signifying the three links of the necklace: springtime, delight, and grace (see Example 21).

This chain of chords in the right hand is in mode 3, first transposition; at the same time the vocal line sings the theme in mode 2, second transposition. Piano, left hand, plays in mode 2, second transposition. The theme is polymodal, with all the notes of the piano, upper staff, belonging to third mode, first transposition, and superimposed on piano, lower staff, where

Example 21. *Poèmes pour Mi,* "Le collier," measures 1–10

all the notes belong to mode 2, second transposition. Example 21 provides an illustration of polymodal modulation. Note that at measure 5 (starred in the example) Messiaen moves mode 2, second transposition, to the upper staff of the piano, where he superimposes it on mode 3, first transposition in left hand. This second polymodality is an inversion of the preceding one, which Messiaen describes as one means of polymodal modulation.[2] At measure 9 the modes form a new inversion and the first polymodality occurs again as at the beginning.

Messiaen has certain chordal harmonies that provide his progressions to different modes or for cadential formulas. In this instance, note that the first chord, bars 1 and 5, lower staff of the piano, is identical to both modes and forms a connection to move smoothly from one mode to the other.

Example 22. A connection of chords, *Technique*, Example 258

In Example 20 the chord in the left hand belongs to mode 2, second transposition, and also to mode 3, first transposition. The upper staff chord A belongs to mode 3, first transposition; chord B belongs to mode 2, second transposition.

The rhythmic emphasis of the first five bars is also important to consider. Messiaen rarely mentions accent except in his discussions of the four categories of notation. In *Poèmes pour Mi* his use of the added value helps to make the phrases and accent points more flexible, a natural expression. Messiaen has formulated one rhythmic concept in which accent plays an important part, called preparation, accent, and descent.[3] A rhythmic preparation leads to the accent, and a rhythmic descent follows it. An illustrated pattern of preparation, accent, and descent is in the first phrase of "Le collier." The letter w marks the accent, x the rhythmic descent, and y the preparation (elongated in measure 4, see Example 21). Added values such as an added note or a dot may lengthen either the preparation for an accent or the rhythmic descent after the accent. To accelerate a descent Messiaen would shorten the value. This placement of accent in the theme shifts the emphasis from what appears to be a pattern of three eighth notes so that it is more sensitive to the vocal line. At the second y (measure 4) the preparation for the next accent (w, measure 5) is much more graceful and leisurely.

Notable also in this example is a more evident use of rhythmic influences to construct an overall rhythmic pattern. The rhythm of the entire first theme (piano part) consists of three varieties of Greek rhythm patterns (see Example 21, measures 6 through 8). The rhythms, named according to number, are:

     1. (. . .)   Tribrach   (.equals short)

     2. (-.)   Trochée   (- equals long)

     3. (-.---) Epitrite II

In measure 8, left hand, notice the inexact augmentation (also bracketed) of the trochée rhythm. In later works, Messiaen used the term "irrational values" to indicate the variation of preexisting Greek or Hindu pattern by augmentation or diminution. The purpose in many cases is to transform the musical quality where accelerando or rallentando is desired. By making one unit smaller than the other, Messiaen can accelerate or slow the passage. In this instance, the sixteenth-note value causes a slight acceleration of the vocal line and the accompaniment.

Proceeding to the last phrase of the theme (measures 11 through 13), both voice and piano are together in mode 7, first transposition, for the climactic phrase. Considering that the preparation for accent (y) occurred in the previous bar, the accent falls on the first eighth note (x); the entire remainder of the phrase is a very graceful rhythmic descent (see Example 23).

Example 23. *Poèmes pour Mi,* theme, measures 11–13

In an examination of the piano part, one can see an interpretation of the Hindu rhythm, râgavardhana, divisible into two fragments (q and r):

Râgavardhana

Interpretation (measure 11)

In measure 12 the rhythm râgavardhana repeats and varies; q loses its last eighth note, while the third quarter note of fragment r adds a dot. This dot, or added value, indicated by a cross, serves to retard the rhythmic descent, thus rendering a more graceful phrase.

One can see, then that in the early works of the second period such as *Poèmes pour Mi,* the usual purpose and effect of the added values is to stretch or diminish the time values in passages that are otherwise basically metrical.

Notable also in measure 11 is the chord on which the accent falls. This is a typical use of the added sixth to a chord, one of Messiaen's preferred harmonies. Here it is added to a B^7 chord, unless one considers it an appoggiatura chord (bracketed in q).

Messiaen speaks of the relation of added notes to chords and values added to rhythms in *Technique.* He believes that the added notes have a certain "citizenship" in the chord, which, of course, they do today. Regarding the appeal these notes and values have for him, Messiaen says:

The same charm, one somewhat perverse, is found in these values of supplement, which make the rhythms limp deliciously, and in these foreign notes which insidiously transform the tint of the chord. [4]

Moving to B section, the commentary begins with a motive using the minor third, an integral part of the entire piece. Also in the melodic contour is the favored tritone (ascending augmented fourth). These intervals form a diminished triad in arpeggio. The modal color of this section derives from mode 7, third transposition, in both voice and piano. As the vocal line describes the necklace with three attributes of the beloved, the melodic contour of ascending minor third and tritone (three notes) repeats in sequence a minor third higher. At measures 17 and 18 is an example of rhythmic preparation, accent, and descent. In the commentary section (measures 14 through 18), tension builds from the motif, moving to an extension of the motif, the motif in sequence, and further extension of the motif with melismatic effect.

Other characteristic features of Messiaen's techniques in composition that may be found in "Le collier" are his non-retrogradable rhythms (see chapt. 7 for illustration) and Greek rhythms (see chapt. 9).

In the final phrase of section *B* a series of chords begins, which contain all degrees of the C-sharp major scale. Messiaen calls this a "chord on the dominant" and provides, in his terms, "an effect of a stained-glass window,"[5] with dissonance and resolution at the same instant. Here one might compare the chords to the poetic imagery of a linking or chain effect. The series of chords repeat for five measures (19 through 23).

At measure 24, a long leisurely descent follows a rhythmic accent on the first half-note of the measure. Again, the word rosettes *(cocasses)* provides a melismatic descent with a long vocalise on the second syllable. The added values at the + sign elongate the descent, begun at x, repated at y, and, once again, with further stretching of the phrase at z (measure 26) (see Example 24). This passage (measures 24 through 26) serves as a transitional and modulatory phrase leading back to *A* section. The vocal

Example 24. *Poèmes pour Mi,* transition to *A* section, measures 24–26

modulation moves from mode 7, fourth transposition (measure 24), to mode 7, third transposition (measure 25), to mode 2, second transposition (measure 26). This last measure reflects the original mode of the vocal part and piano part, left hand, which will repeat in the returning section *A.*

The chords of this passage are quartal and quintal, with each measure ending on the half diminished ninth. The first chord in each measure moves down the minor third.

This elongated rallentando and decrescendo passage brings us to a repeat of *A* section, with fresh lyrics continuing the symbolic imagery and polymodality: mode 2, third transposition, and mode 3, first transposition.

After repetition of the third phrase of the theme (measures 28 and 29), the song finishes with a brief coda. The significant vocal line explaining the necklace occurs here (measure 40 through 45) above a series of polychords. While the melody sustains the final note of the lyric, the modal chords, symbolic of the necklace, continue, gradually diminishing in sound as the piece ends.

The melodic line of the coda begins with the minor third interval in the voice and forms an ascending countour as a contrast to the descending line of the consequent themes.

Harmony in the coda anticipating the reprise of the polymodal final section consists of superimposed triads with roots of each staff, varying degrees apart. The chords consist of major triads and their inversions in the right hand superimposed on alternating minor and major triads in the left hand.

Triads of bars 41 and 42

Upper staff:	E	D	E-flat	D-flat	F
Lower staff:	D	F-sharp	E	D	B

The lower staff line (roots of the chords) belongs to the tones of mode 3, 1, which the left hand played during the theme in the middle modulating section. It leads into an inversion, with this mode moving to the upper right of the piano.

Written during the early second period, this piece is characteristic of Messiaen's compositional technqiues, especially those described in *Technique.* He continues to develop new procedures with his modes of limited transposition, introducing polymodality by superimposition of modes and the modulation of polymodality by inversion of modes. His vocal melodies are sublime; he is outstanding in his ability to write music and lyrics that complement each other. He continues to use added notes to harmony, favored intervals, while he adds new harmony such as the chord on the dominant.

In the area of rhythm, Messiaen's innovations are becoming more integrated into the whole music. He uses Hindu and Greek rhythmic patterns because they provide the musical phrasing he desires for his lyrics. Added rhythmic values appear consistently in the music to add flexibility in the musical lines. Inexact diminution serves a similar purpose, particularly when Messiaen intends to accelerate a phrase. He has added the device called rhythmic preparation, accent, and descent, which provides more tension and relaxation in the musical phrases.

7

Quatuor pour la fin du temps (1941)

War struck France in 1939; Messiaen was soon called to duty as a soldier. His first assignments were as a furniture remover at Sarreguemines, then a hospital attendant at Sarrabbe. Finally, at Verdun he found some musicians with whom he could share mutual interests. Although he was on duty at the front, Messiaen had occasional opportunities to find a church with an organ on which he could indulge himself with avant-garde improvisations.

After only a few months of service, Messiaen was captured by the Germans and taken to a camp near Nancy. There, in the midst of thirty thousand troops, Messiaen noticed an intelligent young soldier who was observing him as well. The two captives lost no time in discovering their mutual musical interests; this brief meeting with Guy Bernard-Delapierre had important consequences for Messiaen. During the night, Messiaen was moved to Germany; he left his name and telephone number near the sleeping Delapierre before his departure.

The duration of Messiaen's captivity was spent in Silesia at Stalag 8A. This was the scene of the composition and first performance of the well-known work *Quatuor pour la fin du temps* (1941). The creation of this compellingly beautiful work came about in the following way.

When he was taken prisoner, Messiaen had managed to keep with him some music paper and scores including the Brandenberg Concerti of Bach, *Les Noces* of Stravinsky, and the Lyric Suite of Berg. Probably because he was able to keep in touch with music, Messiaen was not imprisoned in spirit. At the very least these scores provided him with the means of sustaining psychological good health.

Also at the prison camp were a clarinetist and a violinist who had managed to keep their instruments with them. Eventually, the Germans provided a three-string cello for another prisoner. For these players Messiaen wrote a short trio which later became the fourth movement of

Quatuor. Although there was no piano available, Messiaen continued to compose the entire work for these four instruments. Finally, after completion of the work, an upright piano was brought into the camp. Although it was sadly out of tune and had many keys that stuck, Messiaen rehearsed the group and prepared the work for presentation.

The first performance of *Quatuor* took place in the prison camp on January 15, 1941. The audience included 5,000 prisoners who were workers, peasants, priests, doctors, intellectuals—people from every station in life. The music created a total communication among all who were there. Messiaen has said regarding his premiere of *Quatuor* that his music has never been listened to with such attention and understanding as on that day. In spite of being confined to a combination of instruments he might not ordinarily have chosen, he obtained quite awesome effects from the instruments individually as well as in combination.

The interpretation of the title is twofold. The idea for the work originates in the *Apocalypse*—the last book of the New Testament, or the Revelation of Saint John the Divine—in which the Angel "lifted up his right hand toward heaven and swore an oath . . . that there should be no more Time" (10:5.6). One can contemplate the literal interpretation of this passage; but the reference to time also expresses Messiaen's own philosophical views with regard to musical time, particularly his need to abolish the equal and divisive durational time of traditional music. In the preface to this work he mentions that the "rhythms in each measure contribute to an elongation of time."

Messiaen describes the musical language of the work as

. . . essentially ethereal. It is spiritual and universal. The modes harmoniously and melodically realize ubiquitous tonality and they approach the listener from the eternity of outer space and infinity.[1]

Quatuor consists of eight movements. Seven would appear to be the perfect number if one considers that the creation of the world by God occurred in six days and on the seventh day He rested. According to Messiaen's interpretation, however, this seventh day of repose extends itself into eternity, becoming the eighth day that represents unalterable peace and eternal light.

Several movements from this work are worthy of close examination. For full appreciation of the ethereal language of this composition, which carries the listener to the "eternity of infinity," the eighth movement, "Louange à l'immortalité de Jésus" for violin and piano is a necessary and unforgettable listening experience. The sixth movement, "Danse de la fureur, pour les sept trompettes" is of interest rhythmically and very effective musically. The "Liturgie de cristal" contains innovations that foreshadow later developments in technique, as well as characteristics in aspects of rhythm, melody, and harmony.

In the song cycles such as *Poèmes pour Mi* the piano and voice are rhythmically interdependent and blend as one instrument. *Quatuor* marks a turning point in its polyrhythmic structures, which Messiaen went on to use in many later works. "Liturgie de cristal" is the most representative movement from this viewpoint in its use of polyrhythm and panisorhythm.[2]

In the score Messiaen has written "Liturgue de cristal" in fourth notation. This means that he has written in a normal meter a rhythm that has no relation to it. This is necessary when several musicians perform a work, particularly when it contains superimposition of several different rhythms. The notation is "false," since it contradicts the rhythmic conception of the composer. When the indicated accents are performed, however, the listener hears the true rhythm. For example, Messiaen has selected from the first movement a passage in the clarinet part that he has notated in first and fourth notation.[3] In Example 25 the first musical line illustrates the composer's conception in first notation, without regular measure or beat.

Example 25. *Quatuor pour la fin du temps,* first movement, measures 6 through 8

The barlines refer only to phrase endings, accent emphasis, or the change of accidentals. The second line of Example 25 is the same passage written in fourth notation, and appears as it is in the score. It realizes Messiaen's rhythmic intention if the musicians observe the notated accents. This notation is easier for a group of musicians to perform correctly when playing together.

"Liturgie de cristal" is the first selection in which Messiaen introduced birdsong. The clarinet part represents the song of the merlin at daybreak. This melodic line is independent rhythmically throughout the piece. Using

Example 26. *Quatuor,* first movement, clarinet part, measures 1–3

all twelve scale tones, the line does not follow serial methods but is improvisatory in the style of the merlin's song.

The form of this single melodic line follows a structural pattern of theme and commentary. The ensuing variations of both present a forerunner of the compositional procedure that led to the couplet-refrain and other strophic forms used by Messiaen in his later birdsong compositions. Most important here are the extensive variations of theme and commentary, allowing for the improvisational nature of the birdsong.

Each instrumental melody moves independently of the other melodic lines. The clarinet part follows this outline:

a—theme	(measures 1–2)
b—commentary	(measures 3–7)
a'—theme	(measures 7–11)
b'—commentary	(measures 11–18)
a^2—theme	(measures 19–21)
b^2—commentary	(measures 21–34)
Coda	(measures 34–42)

The coda is a further development of commentary material using many ascending leaps and chromatic movement upward. The clarinet melody gives the impression to the listener of the music moving away beyond the tops of the trees, to infinity.

An interesting feature in the first two measures of Example 26 are three simple non-retrogradable rhythms in succession. (See palindromic rhythms in brackets, first two measures, Example 26.)

Example 27. *Quatuor,* first movement, violin part, measures 13–15

The violin, which represents birdsong, begins with staccato notes at the tip of the bow and includes the use of a two-note tremolo of rapid repetition of the tritone in a very high register. This violin part forms a secondary counterpoint to the principal melody in the clarinet. It is modal, belonging to mode 3, fourth transposition, and functions independently of the other musical parts.

This violin melody, based on the repetition and variation of first and second statements, is improvisatory. The first statement (theme, measures 1 through 11) consists of rapid staccato, repeated notes; rests, which contribute to the birdsong-like pattern; and the three-note arc contour, which contains the tritone. The commentary also uses this fragment (measures 11 through 15) and builds its statement from the tremolo, rapid repetition of the tritone and descending chromatic movement. These components of the violin part vary in an improvisational manner according to the following structural pattern:

a—theme	(measures 1–11)
b—commentary	(measures 11–15)
a'—theme	(measures 16–25)
b'—commentary	(measures 28–32)
*a*²—theme	(measures 33–35)
*b*²—commentary	(measures 36–42)

It is apparent that the pattern once again moves independently in melody and rhythm from the birdsong in the clarinet part. It is independent also from the other two instrumental parts.

Superimposed on these two birdsongs are two independent rhythmic pedals played by the cello and the piano. These rhythmic pedals, combined with independent melodic or harmonic ostinatos, suggest isorhythm and reflect Messiaen's interest in techniques of other historical periods. The device demonstrates also his preference of methods that coincide with his desire to organize rhythm as an independent musical element.

The piano's rhythmic pedal consists of a repeated pattern of seventeen durations; this composite rhythm pattern constitues a tâla. The most important tâla used in Messiaen's compositions, it appears in several major works. Constructed from three Çârngadeva rhythms: râgavardhana (quoted previously), candrakalâ ♪♩♩ ♩.♩.♩.♩ , and lackskmiça ♪♩. ♩ ♩ . It appears in rhythmic pedal as shown in Example 28.

Example 28. Three Çârngadeva rhythms

The repetition of twenty-nine different chords that appear in the piano part colors this rhythmic pedal of seventeen rhythmic values. Because the number of rhythmic values totals seventeen, and the number of chords twenty-nine, the harmony transforms into unusual rhythmic variants as it repeats five and one-half times during the entire work. The possible combinations involving these elements are innumerable and Messiaen does not extend the work to explore all of them. Nor do they form its structure beyond providing unity for the free patterns of the birdsong that shape the piece. The pedals do resemble the isorhythmic structure that provided formal organization in the motets of the fourteenth century.

In the cello part, marked with the letter A, the rhythmic pedal repeats one and one-quarter times during the piece.

Example 29. *Quatuor,* first movement, cello part, measures 1–8

The cello tâla, or rhythmic pedal, divides into two non-retrogradable patterns. See Example 30, A and B.

Example 30. Non-retrogradable rhythm patterns

At B, the two groups bracketed, with another bracket and a plus sign denote the common central value. Messiaen states in *Technique* that the common central value is actually a half note divided into four eighth notes, which is also non-retrogradable.[4]

The cello part, played in harmonics, sounds two octaves higher than the lower notes, which helps to unify the timbres of this small group of instruments not ordinarily combined in this manner. The cello's melodic pedal consists of five tones in the whole-tone scale, repeated in the same order throughout. The resulting overlap of notes and durations produces different rhythmic values for the melodic repetitions. The whole tone scale pattern in the cello part recurs twenty-one times.

These two isorhythmic patterns in the cello and piano parts continue from beginning to the end. Since both isorhythmic parts appear simultaneously, we can call the technique panisorhythm.

The harmonic pedal in the piano part, independent of the melodies surrounding it, bears examination for its harmonies as an independent entity. The pedal (twenty-nine chords) contains the following harmonic pattern with each repetition:

1. Chords on the dominant with appoggiaturas extending through the first eight chords. This means that further appoggiaturas are added to the original chord, containing all the notes of the diatonic scale; so that the chord becomes a resolution of a more complex dissonance.[5]

2. Chords consisting of minor ninths and elevenths making up the next seven chords; the roots of this chord passage contain tones of mode 3, third transposition.

3. A passage of six chords in third mode, third transposition.

4. Another series of six chords in mode 2, second transposition.

The two rhythmic pedals end abruptly at the end of the movement where the birdsong fades. Messiaen creates here a musical expression of movement into infinity. He interprets the silence following the movement as the "silence of the heavens."[6]

Quatuor pour la fin du temps is an important work in Messiaen's development. It not only illustrates his creative genius functioning under very difficult circumstances, but provides a continuing link to the past and the future. In "Liturgie de cristal" his modal writing included mode 1 (whole-tone scale), which he rarely used; he also used the modes in alternation in the piano part (modes 2 and 3). Harmonic features include the chord on the dominant. Most notable in this movement is the introduction of birdsong, the principal melody played by the clarinet and the additional soft melody played by the violin.

"Liturgie de cristal" is most innovative because of its rhythmic interest. The movement contains non-retrogradable rhythms that link it with previous works. Added features are the use of Indian rhythmic patterns (tâla) in the piano part and the use of simultaneous rhythmic pedals, or panisorhythm, which appear in the cello and piano parts. By combining the rhythmic pedal of seventeen values with a harmonic pedal of twenty-nine chords, Messiaen created autonomous rhythm and harmony. Since the alignment of rhythm and harmony shifts continually, the result is the liberation of one element from the other.

8

Vingt regards sur l'Enfant Jésus (1944)

After the war Messiaen returned to Paris and in 1942 resumed his teaching career with an appointment as Professor of Harmony at the Paris Conservatory. Also returned to Paris was Guy Bernard-Delapierre, with whom Messiaen had formed a brief friendship on the first day of his captivity. At Delapierre's invitation, Messiaen taught a private course in composition in the former's home. This course, begun in 1943, covered the formal, orchestral, melodic, harmonic, and rhythmic analysis of all kinds of music, including ancient, classical, romantic, and modern. Messiaen's new class attracted many illustrious students, including Pierre Boulez, Yvonne Loriod, Jean-Louis Martinet, and Karlheinz Stockhausen. A number of these students went on to achieve great distinction in their own music careers. During the years since organizing this composition class, Messiaen has always spoken of his first students with love and affection. They, in turn, have expressed respect, paying homage to Messiaen throughout their careers, always commending the methods by which he gave them their start. Because of his aid and encouragement to so many students who pursued their own directions in music, Messiaen has been called father of the avant garde. These students chose to call themselves *Les flèches* ("the arrows"), indicating their hope of shooting arrows into the future.

It was at this time that Messiaen wrote his important theoretical work, *Technique de mon langage musical* (1944), and dedicated it to Guy Bernard-Delapierre, who had helped him to begin the type of course he most loved to teach. The purpose of the book, in two volumes, was to answer the many questions asked by his students regarding his own techniques of composition.

77

The period of the early 1940s was not only important for the development of Messiaen's teaching career, but was a crucially formative time for composing. Having found a superlative pianist and interpreter of music for the piano in his pupil Yvonne Loriod, Messiaen was inspired to write two major works for the instrument, *Visions de l'Amen* (1943) and *Vingt regards sur l'Enfant Jésus* (1944). Later he wrote *Catalogue d'oiseaux* for piano (see chapt. 12), and he featured the piano as a prominent instrument in many orchestral works after that time. Yvonne Loriod has remained the foremost interpreter of Messiaen's piano music, continuing the long association that began with his first composition class.

Vingt regards sur l'Enfant Jésus means more than the literal translation of "twenty gazes upon the infant Jesus." A better definition for the word *regards* is "contemplation"; the twenty movements in this work involve the contemplation of the Child of God by God the Father, the Church, the Holy Spirit, the Virgin, angels, wise men, and immaterial or symbolic entities that include Time, the Star, the Cross, and Silence. In the seventeenth movement, "Regard du silence," Silence symbolizes Heaven where the peace of God surpasses understanding. Messiaen describes this section in the preface to the score, ". . . silence in the hand, reversed rainbow, each silence of the manger reveals music and colors that are the mysteries of Jesus Christ."[1]

Messiaen gives credit to several writers for their influence on this work, especially Dom Columba Marmion *(Christ and His Mysteries)* and Maurice Toesca *(Les douze regards).* [2] He also discusses the arrangement of the subjects according to number symbolism. Although Messiaen attaches prime importance to Christian symbolism here and in other works written between 1928 and 1944, he has stated that it is theological rather than mystical.[3] The religious sources and Christian symbolism inspired Messiaen and determined the ordering of the twenty movements. Symbolism also has an influence on the melodic and harmonic shape of *Vingt regards* through the use of cyclic themes that function symbolically within the context of the work.

The first one is the *thème de Dieu* ("theme of God"), which appears in complete form in the first piece, "Regard du Père." This piece is No. 1 in the cycle because the Father is the first person of the Trinity. The *thème de Dieu* occurs again in Nos. V, VI, X, XI, and XV.

The second cyclic theme is the *thème de l'étoile et de la Croix* ("theme of the star and of the Cross"). This symbolizes the star that proclaimed the birth of Christ and the cross on which he died. It appears in the second piece, "Regard de l'étoile," as well as No. VII, "Regard de la Croix."

The third cyclic theme, *thème d'accords* ("theme of chords" or "harmony") does not function symbolically. It provides a unifying factor throughout the work. This theme appears in the analysis of "Regard du silence," where it is highlighted.

An important compositional technique developed in this movement is a process called *agrandissement asymétrique.* It is similar to the technique, previously described, of *personnages rythmiques.* One concerns rhythmic changes; the other involves pitch. In *agrandissement asymétrique,* a theme or passage is repeated several times. Some groups of notes in the passage remain the same, while Messiaen transposes other groups upward, and still others of notes downward.

"Regard du silence" contains the third cyclic theme; it also contains the technique of *agrandissement asymétrique.* Furthermore, Messiaen has used several other devices such as rhythmic canon, polymodality, augmentation, and so on, in creating the effect of "music of the silence"; this selection is highly representative of many characteristic features.

The music of the silence depicts the aura of the silence surrounding the sleeping child. Messiaen uses his modal harmonies in creating mosaic effects of colors often juxtaposed into recognizable patterns to give structure to the piece. The sections contribute their own impressions to the total picture and reflect thematic content.

The format outlines sections without labeling themes as such. Later in the analysis, after the discussion of various features, we repeat the format using descriptive phrases and specifying modes of the sections.

Formal outline of "Regard du silence"

Introduction   (measures 1–19)

Section *A*   (measures 20–36)

    a—(measures 20–29)
    b—(measures 30–36)

Section *B*   (measures 37–40)

    c—(measure 37)
    d—(measures 38–39)
    e—(measure 40)

Section *C*   (measures 41–52)

    f—(measures 41–52)

Section *A'*   (measures 53–71)

    a'—(measures 53–62)
    b'—(measures 63–71)

Section *B'*   (measures 72–75)

    c'—(measure 72)
    d'—(measures 73–74)
    e'—(measure 75)

Section *C'*   (measures 76–88)

    f'—(measures 76–88)

Coda   (measures 89–110)

One might view the entire work in a rather symmetrical fashion, as in Figure 1.

Figure 1. Formal outline of "Regard du silence"

Introduction	Section *A*	Section *B*	Section *C*	
	ab	*cde*	*fg*	
	Section *A'*	Section *B'*	Section *C'*	
	a'b'	*c'd'e'*	*f'g'*	Coda

The three central sections repeat with the same structure, however, each repetition varies the original material so that the repetition resembles a variational technique. The introduction and coda become symmetrical in performance, even though the coda is twice as long because of the tempo markings that direct it to be played more than twice as quickly.

The piece begins with a two-part harmonic canon that extends through bar 19. This canon is also polymodal with upper staff in third mode, fourth transposition, and lower staff in fourth mode, fourth transposition.

As we have seen in other selections, Messiaen may augment or diminish patterns by the addition or subtraction of a *chronos protos* unit.[4] In movement 17 he has produced the rhythmic canon by augmentation, that is, by the addition of a dot to each rhythmic value in the upper staff. The new rhythmic pattern becomes the pattern of the lower staff (see Example 31). Brackets mark the repetition of the entire pattern in the upper staff, as in

Example 31. *Vingt regards,* "Regard du silence," measures 1–8

Example 31. In the introduction of this movement (measures 1 through 19) the entire passage of seventeen chords occurs three times in the upper staff, combined in the lower staff with two repetitions of seventeen different chords. The successive durations have alphabetical markings in each voice to assist in rhythmic comparison since the chords in each pattern are not the same.

At the end of the rhythmic canon (introduction), section *A* begins with chords of the same polymodality as the canon using the tritone as well as perfect fourths. These chords lead into the first appearance of the third cyclic theme in this selection, the *thème d'accords,* which appears in measure 22. This theme, previously defined, is a unifying factor in the entire work. In some movements it occurs in its original form; in others it is fragmentary. In measures 22 and 23 it is concentrated into two repeated chords rather than the four of the original presentation (see Example 32).

Example 32. Third cyclic theme, *thème d'accords*

Examples of the technique of augmentation by addition of a dot, as well as inexact diminution, may be found throughout "Regard du silence." When Messiaen uses inexact diminution, the ratio becomes unequal. He says that "very inexact augmentations or diminutions might also be termed rhythmic variants."[5]

In *b* part of *A* section (measures 30 through 36), the modal colors shift to mode 2, third transposition in all three staves of the piano. Using symmetrical ascending arpeggios from this mode, consisting of minor thirds, perfect and augmented fourths, and a minor seventh, this passage moves with rallentando motion into the next section.

Section *B* (measure 37) introduces another shift in modal colors. This entire section is more lively and gives rapidly changing coloristic impressions; the first, a cascade of descending chords in mode 3. This chord passage moves immediately into a polymodal passage of arpeggios in contrary motion (measures 38 through 39). The pentatonic effect in the top voice (measure 37) reflected in the left hand motif (measure 38) is of interest. The rhythm pattern of the arpeggios is six against eight; the modes are fourth mode, first transposition, superimposed on seventh mode, third transposition.

The arpeggios, both hands in the treble register, shift next to another coloristic pattern of symmetrical arpeggios in the second mode (measure 40). In the right hand Messiaen superimposes a C-major arpeggio over an A-flat dominant seventh arpeggio, which builds rapidly in a crescendo to *f* at the highest degree of the arpeggio, followed by a pause.

The mood of the sweeping arpeggios changes abruptly with the beginning of the next section *C* as the cyclic *thème d'accords* returns. This time Messiaen presents it *en arc en ciel* ("rainbow") (see music in Example 33).

Messiaen obtains the rainbow color effect by combining the *thème d'accords,* moving to the right in the regular manner, with its retrograde, in the upper staff. Numbers 1, 2, 3, and 4 in Example 33 mark the regular

Example 33. *Thème d'accords* (rainbow effect), measures 41–44

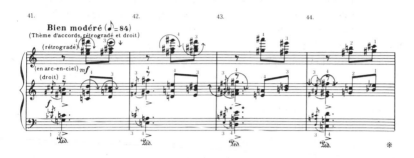

order of the four chords of *thème d'accord;* the retrograde pattern appears as two chords together in the upper and middle staves, numbered 4, 3, 4, 3 and 4, 3, 2, 1. The regular pattern occurs in the lower and middle staves according to numbered chords, including appoggiatura chords.

In this four measures there is also a noncomplicated and clear example of the process *agrandissement asymétrique.* As the cyclic theme repeats, Messiaen has transposed various chords or notes of chords up a semitone or whole step. Example 33 illustrates these chords by marking the note or chord with an arc, arrow pointing upward. Other notes or chords move down a tone or semitone (marked with an arc, arrow point downward). Unmakred notes in the example remain the same at the repetition. Some chords consist of inversions of the original chord in the theme, for example, starred chord, measure 43 of Example 33.

The combined *thème d'accord* and its retrograde lead into musical material that is indicative of later birdsong (measures 45 through 52). The modes here have returned to mode 3, third transposition (measures 45 through 57) and then into the polymodal color of modes 3 and 4, evident in the opening rhythmic canon as well as in the opening chords of section *A*.

Reiterating softly the tone G, the music suddenly plunges into a forte repeat of the first inner section (*A'*, measure 53). Chords become *ff* in the polymodal context of the first two measures of this section, until suddenly in measure 55 the *thème d'accords* reappears softly. The theme is a concentrated version with two chords in the one measure. In measure 56 the first chord repeats with the appoggiatura.

In the varied reprise of sections *A, B,* and *C,* we discuss only the variations of the material already presented. Section *A (a)* repeats the earlier material with the exception of the last three measures (60 through 62). These three measures, although in the same mode 3, are in reverse order from the earlier section (measure 27 through 29). In the second part of *A* section *(b),* the arpeggios retain the color of mode 2, second transposition; but here they have moved up an augmented fourth from the original version. At the end of this section there is a rhythmic descent, extended by the addition of two measures (68 and 69) to the rubato phrase that originally ended section *A.*

Section *B'* (measure 72) contains a restatement of material in part *c* (measure 37); this time, however, it is a passage of ascending chords. The colors of mode 3 are still used, although in retrograde form with this repetition. Messiaen presents remaining chords at the end of the passage in a different order in inversion. This procedure he has termed "interversion."[6]

Arriving at the sweeping passages of arpeggios (measures 73 and 74), once again the arpeggios contain the same intervals and belong to the same combination of modes (modes 4 and 7), although the intervals have moved up a fifth. This results in different transpositions of the modes: mode 4 has moved from the first to second transposition (right hand); mode 7 has moved from the third to fourth transposition (left hand).

The larger arcs of arpeggios, part *c',* have also moved up a fifth, although remaining in mode 2; thereby sounding the G-major arpeggio superimposed over the E-flat seventh arpeggio in a polytonal effect. Dynamics markings are identical in both the original and the repeated sections.

The *thème d'accords* repeats at section *C',* combined with its retrograde (measures 76 through 79). The same transpositions of individual notes and chords, some upward, some downward, remain constant here.

In the following passage (measures 80 through 88) the material remains the same as the original until measure 84, when a shift up a minor third occurs. Throughout the next three measures Messiaen modulates to complete the entire section one whole step lower. The F tone, repeated rather than G in measures 87 and 88, links this section with the chain of chords that open and close the piece.

The coda, beginning at measure 89, compares harmonically and modally to the opening or introductory material in this selection. Once again in mode 3, fourth transposition (right hand), combined with mode 4, fourth transposition (left hand), the chords are typical harmonies from these modes, repeating patterns from the chords at the beginning. At measure 89 a rhythmic pedal replaces the canon, using four chords in the left hand, with twelve repetitions (see Example 34). In the right hand, seventeen

Example 34. *Vingt regards,* "Regard du silence," coda, measures 89–90

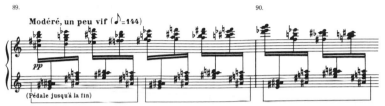

chords complete their cycle three times until the two hands reach the middle of measure 95. A rising harmonic line, which had begun with an ascending and descending chord pattern in the right hand, now increases tension with new ascending chords and inversions from the same mode. The rising line breaks off abruptly, to begin once more with increasing tension at measure 96. The ascent begins, then gradually unwinds (measure 97), and descends to the starting chord of the seventeen-chord pattern that has risen one octave higher (measure 98).

The rhythmic pedal begins anew in both hands; this time the left hand joins the right hand in continuing the chord pattern an octave higher. The upper staff completes one group of seventeen chords, as the lower staff continues the pedal of four chords. Now the varied pattern, which had started in measures 95 and 96, begins once more. Moving up in the higher ascending spiral, the pattern (measure 100) begins again in an ascending line and breaks abruptly to start once more, eliminating a chord at the starting point.

Having reached a high point, a new contour of chords is begun, continually beginning with the highest chord and descending slightly. With each repetition, new chords are introduced into the pattern at midway points between the highest and lowest chords.

After increasing the tension and sonorities in this manner, the last new chord to be added (measure 103) begins a new and final pattern in measure 104, which consists of four chords in each hand repeated in a new rhythmic pedal. The new pattern still contains harmonies belonging to mode 3, fourth transposition, and mode 4, fourth transposition. This pedal extends for seven measures, gradually diminishing in intensity and tempo. By the final measure (110) the intensity has faded to four pianissimos; the last chord of the rhythmic pedal extends briefly over an extended silence, allowing the vibrations of many resounding chords to complete their reverberations and blend into that silence.

The following outline repeats the original format; this time using descriptive phrases to indicate the various sections, as well as specifying the modes used:

Formal outline of Vingt regards

Introduction—rhythmic canon	modes 3, 4 and 4,4

Section A—(transition, a and b)

a—*thème d'accord*	mode 3
b—arpeggio passage	mode 2

Section B—(parts c, d, e)

c—descending chord passage	mode 3
d—arpeggios in contrary motion	modes 4 and 7
e—symmetrical arpeggios	mode 2

Section C—(parts f and g)

f—*thème d'accord* and retrograde	
g—birdsong material	modes 3 and 4

Section A'—(varied reprise of parts a and b)

a'—*thème d'accord*	mode 3
b'—arpeggio passage (up a tritone)	mode 2

Section B'—(varied reprise of parts c'd' and e')

c'—ascending chord passage	mode 3
d'—arpeggios in contrary motion (up a fifth)	modes 4 and 7
e'—symmetrical arpeggios (up a fifth)	mode 2

Section C'—(varied reprise of parts f' and g')

f'—*thème d'accord* and retrograde	
g'—birdsong material (modulation)	modes 3 and 4
Coda—rhythmic pedal	modes 3 and 4

In *Vingt regards* Messiaen has developed important processes that were begun in earlier works. He changes the modes frequently during a piece;

he often superimposes different modes, creating polymodality. In "Regard du silence" he creates a shifting tonality and a sense of modulation with the use of various modes (3, 4, 2, and 7). Other movements in this work keep the same tonal center although the modes change.

The technique of rhythmic pedal is apparent in "Regard du silence." Messiaen's use of augmentation by the addition of a dot is an important factor in the two-part harmonic rhythmic canon at the very beginning of the piece. Other features that appear are the rhythmic technique of inexact diminution and the development of the process of *agrandissement asymétrique.*

Messiaen uses cyclic themes in *Vingt regards* to provide a unifying factor. In "Regard du silence" the third cyclic theme *(thème d'accords)* appears in concentrated form and also simultaneously with its retrograde to form a rainbow effect. His use of Christian symbolism is apparent in the definition of cyclic themes as well as in the order of numbers of the twenty movements.

All of the techniques that have appeared earlier show the growth and maturity in Messiaen's creative development. They also provide the continuous link in the evolution of his art. In the area of new innovation, most striking is his writing for the piano. Of the twentieth-century composers, Messiaen stands almost alone in his accomplishment of transforming the technique and expression of this instrument.

9

Cinq rechants (1949)

On April 21, 1945, the premiere of *Trois petites liturgies de la présence divine* (1944) was presented by the Orchestre de la Société des Concerts du Conservatoire, directed by Roger Désormière, the Yvonne Gouverné Chorale, with Yvonne Loriod, pianist, and Ginette Martenot playing the Ondes Martenot. The work had been commissioned by Mme. Denise Tual for the concerts of the Pléiade. The premiere, an immediate success with the public, caused one of the greatest critical debacles of Messiaen's entire career.

The extremely negative reaction to the work of certain of his colleagues and critics amazed Messiaen, and he was still searching for explanations years afterwards. Although it was bold in its musical esthetic as well as its combination of timbres, this did not seem to him to justify such rage. Messiaen has indicated in interviews that the criticism was motivated largely by the attackers' ignorance of the texts of the Holy Scriptures that he had used. In addition, the orchestral composition was out of the ordinary. These are two possible reasons, not necessarily justifiable, why some critics (possibly the well-meaning, conservative types), heaped insults on the head of the composer. Certainly Messiaen has not been exempt from the vilification that twentieth-century composers have received with each new step they have taken. In the case of *Petites liturgies* the abuse came entirely from critics; the public embraced the work from the beginning. In a few short years it had been performed in many places and quickly passed its hundredth performance.

Shortly after the premiere of this work, a group of musicians led by Pierre Boulez went to Claude Delvincourt, current director of the Paris Conservatory to persuade him to put Messiaen on the faculty. Delvincourt was very much in sympathy with Messiaen's work and his teachings, but he realized that he must move carefully if an appointment was to be a lasting one. It was obvious that due to the current uproar and controversy surrounding Messiaen's latest work, the advisors to the government minister in charge would disapprove of allowing such an upstart to influence composition students at the Conservatory. Delvincourt knew also that the senior professors would be disturbed; most of them considered Messiaen to be crazy.

In a clever move, Delvincourt suggested to the board that Messiaen teach a class in analysis. He noted that this would pacify the students who were petitioning for Messiaen, and suggested that interest in the class would soon fade away. In truth, Delvincourt foresaw that Messiaen's course would be highly successful, and his maneuvers paid off in the long run. Messiaen began his famous class in analysis at the Conservatory, replacing the initial course that met in Guy Bernard-Delapierre's home. Although it has since been called by several names, such as esthetics, musical philosophy, and musical analysis, it has always been a class in analysis similar to the independent one begun in 1943. Messiaen had firmly established his reputation as a teacher in France.

With the works following *Vingt regards* and *Trois petites liturgies,* a new phase of composition emphasized mythological symbolism rather than specifically Christian symbolism. It is focused on the Tristan and Isolde myth, particularly Wagner's version in which the love-death symbol plays a large part. Between 1945–1950 Messiaen wrote *Harawi,* the *Turangalîla-symphonie,* and *Cinq rechants* as a trilogy on the subject of love and death. Linked with the mythology in *Cinq rechants* is a surrealistic quality: the work is concerned with the workings of the subconscious; symbols of allegory are used to convey the message; and the objective is to invoke a dream world, where objects not normally associated with each other enter into opposition.

Turangalîla-symphonie contains a wealth of ideas and procedures; any analysis of it must therefore be lengthy. It has complex superimpositions of rhythmic, melodic, and harmonic structures; and represents a culmination of Messiaen's development to that time. The work, one of maximum complexity, emphasizes the significance of the directions taken by works that immediately followed it. The compositions of the next few years became simpler in structure, and contained the fruits of further research into new techniques of rhythm and duration.

Cinq rechants represents new explorations in technique. In this relatively short work Messiaen economically treated aspects of rhythm and dynamics in ways that had a formative influence on his younger contemporaries. The only vocal work to be written over a period of many years, it also illustrates sharply the change and growth in Messiaen's style since the period before the war years when he composed his earlier song cycles. The choral writing for twelve unaccompanied voices is startlingly original, making use of novel technqiues (e.g., a twelve-part canon in Movement III) and moving easily between speech and song.

Since there are rarely sharp lines dividing the periods of any composer's evolution, this work is an important one to include in a representative sampling of Messiaen's work because it is specifically illustrative in connecting past and subsequent compositions. It indicates areas where Messiaen's thought, dependent on collage structures, remains basically unchanged; it contains the symbolism and surrealism of the immediately preceding works; and it clearly illustrates the rhythmic areas previously only touched on. Most important, it foreshadows the rhythmic manipulation, rather than superimposition, that became a significant feature of the next years.

With *Cinq rechants* Messiaen moves away from tonality as previously conceived; he temporarily drops his concentration on birdsong. Written for three sopranos, three contraltos, three tenors, and three basses, all voices perform solo. Messiaen achieves variety of timbre by grouping voices into the normal divisions of register, by dividing them into twelve solo parts in certain movements, or by varying the number of singers on any given single line.

The lyrics are written partly in French and partly in pseudo-Hindi, which Messiaen invented as a means of going beyond ordinary modes of expression. He designed the pseudo-Hindi words carefully, choosing each syllable for the

. . . gentleness or violence of its attack; for its aptitude in giving prominence to musical rhythms. They permit the smooth blending of four elements; phonetic (timbre), dynamic (intensities), kinetic (accents) and quantitative (values).[1]

The structure is based on a form Messiaen describes as "variations of the first theme separated by developments of the second."[2] This form provided a basis for the couplet refrain and other strophic forms of his later music.

Messiaen has used the term "rechant" in recollection of the work *Le printemps* by Claude le Jeune. The *Airs* of Claude le Jeune (1528–1600), one of the most important of the French Renaissance chanson composers, are divided into couplets and refrains, or chants and rechants. Messiaen has used the form and title for this work, but the treatment is somewhat different. Both composers give the rechant the same basic text and music throughout each piece. The chants, however, differ somewhat in that le Jeune used the same music with different text in each repetition. Messiaen's chant or couplet (as indicated in the score) uses the same text, while he varies the music with rhythmic expansion and sometimes, new material.

While le Jeune used the Greek meters exclusively, Messiaen uses not only these but some of the one hundred twenty decî-tâlas from India and related rhythms of his own.

Using repetitive images and recurring refrains, the five movements form a continuous song of love containing richly varied tone colors and references to Tristan and Isolde. The work is also musically linked with *Turangalîla-symphonie* and *Harawi* by the use of thematic material from those works.

Cinq rechants sings of human love. The text and music are nearly inseparable, representing perhaps the most total fusion of any of Messiaen's vocal works. Each of the twelve vocal parts has its own melodic line that places great demands on the abilities and musicianship of the performers.

The forms of the five movements differ in the exact layout of couplets and rechants. Some movements have introductions, some do not; some begin with the couplet and some with the rechant. The format of the second movement, having no introduction, is the following:

Couplet—measures 1–22

Rechant—measures 23–31

Couplet—measures 32–46

Rechant—measures 47–55

Coda—measures 56–62

The substance of the story of Tristan and Isolde, most relevant to *Cinq rechants,* is the lovers' concern only for each other and their heedlessness of Brangaene's warning of approaching dawn. Various movements contain symbolic references to other similar love myths as well.

The second movement, analyzed in this chapter, describes through symbols in its lyric, the calm, peaceful, and happy state of the lovers. First couplet:

My first time, earth, earth, the open fan
My last time, earth, earth, the closed fan
Luminous, my smile of death, my young destiny
(spirit) on the rivers. . . . A solo of the flute
cradles the four lizards . . . while drawing you
away . . .

The composer states in the prefatory notes that the work is a song of life. The words serve only as guides to interpreting the feeling of the poem and the music; the singers should consider the effect of the sound rather than the meaning. Among Messiaen's terms of imagery, *terre* or "earth" is the symbol of the physical being; *etoile*, "star" or "destiny," symbolizes the spiritual being.

The voices in this movement perform in combinations as well as individually. Different registers of the melodic line produce contrast and changes of color and timbre. Contrasting weights of the voices, combinations of vocal quality as well as of the spoken voice with the sung melody all provide unusual variety.

The music consists of a single melodic line throughout the movement combined with ranges of the human voice and altered in unique ways. The melodic style is similar to that of the French troubadors; the setting is syllabic, with occasional short melismatic figures.

The spoken notes (beginning of the reprise of chant) are diamond-shaped. Messiaen has stated in the preface that words of pseudo-Hindi origin (imaginary) should be pronounced phonetically as written. Letters in parentheses are not pronounced.

The notation of this movement is obviously of the second type in Messiaen's categories of notation. The metric changes, occurring in nearly every bar, demand closer examination for indications of the direction of his rhythmic development as well as for indications of the influences supporting that development. It is at this point in Messiaen's creative life that the "variety of rhythmic patterns of ancient Greece," which he cited as an influence in *Technique*,[3] becomes more evident. For this reason, the present analysis considers quite fully particular characteristics of Messiaen's mode of rhythmic expression in terms of their relationships with these metrics.

In chapter 2, section 1 of *Technique*, Messiaen briefly discusses his marked preference for the "rhythms of prime numbers (five, seven, eleven, thirteen, et cetera)," which were among the variety of meters used by the Greeks. He also describes his goal of arriving at an ametrical music, by which he means a music with free but precise rhythmic patterns, as opposed to measures or equally barred music. [4] By the replacement of measure and beat with a short value *(chronos protos)* and the free multiplication of that primary value, Messiaen draws on principles he encountered in the study of ancient metrics, and which he developed in his own theoretical perspectives for writing "music without measure."[5]

The first couplet begins with a contralto solo for four bars; the next line is continued by solo bass (measures 5 through 8). Three sopranos sing the next two bars in unison, whereupon they are joined by one contralto, one tenor, and one bass for the succeeding phrase. In this manner the texture, weight, color, and range are influences throughout the work.

The melodic line is totally chromatic; all twelve tones occur in the first couplet, although they follow no special pattern. The ragged and unusual melodic shape of this work is very different from earlier song cycles, however, one recognizes chromatic formula and the tritone interval that has been favored by Messiaen in so many of his works.

The melody begins with two ascending perfect fourths, one-half step apart. The line moves downward with the tritone interval and chromatic formulas (measure 3) before completing the contralto phrase with an arc made up of a second-inversion triad in arpeggio. The line ends on C natural, the same as the starting note (see Example 35).

Example 35. *Cinq rechants,* No. 2, measures 1–4

In the first phrase of *Cinq rechants,* No. 2, the *chronos protos* (in Greek terminology) is the sixteenth note, or the shortest value that can be multiplied but not divided. The first and second measures contain beats that are composed of two *chronos protos* units for each of the eighth-note counts. The uneven quality of beats in this couplet helps to establish and maintain its interval irregularity. Messiaen has based this rhythm clearly on the original interpretation of Greek principles pertaining to multiplication of the primary unit.

In the first line of Example 35 are clear illustrations of Messiaen's predilection for rhythms using primary numbers. The additions of *chronos protos* in the example, adding up to eleven and thirteen, are marked above the musical line. This melodic line is repeated, an octave lower by the solo bass.

The next part of the couplet section (measures 9 through 12) continues use of the perfect fourth and chromatic formula (measures 9 and 10) sung by three sopranos. The chromatic formula is repeated with a slight extension by the entire group of twelve mixed voices (measures 11 and 12), ending the phrase once more on C.

Example 36. *Cinq rechants*, No. 2, measures 5–12

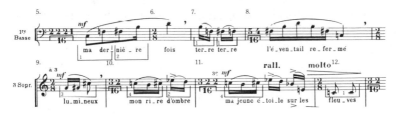

Extract from *Cinq rechants*, II, reproduced with permission. Copyright by Editions Salabert, Paris, France.

The second movement has a number of Greek meters, with some in every basic category of time ratio that existed in ancient times: simple ratio (1:1), double ratio (2:1), and hemiola (3:2). In Example 36 brackets indicate:

1. Spondée rhythm with 1:1 ratio and   ♩ ♩   pattern
2. Trochée rhythm with 2:1 ratio and   ♩ ♪   pattern

Other rhythms that belong to divisions of time in Greek practice include:

3. Anapest (measure 9) with 1:1 ratio and ♫ ♩   pattern
4. Tribrach (measure 10) with 2:1 ratio and ♫ ♪ pattern

Rhythm with a hemiola relationship, that is, 3:2, add to the principle of irregularity that is so typical of ancient Greek metrics. This category of time ratio is represented by:

5. Antibacchic peon (measure 18) with 2:3 ratio and
   ♩ ♩ ♪   pattern

6. Cretic or peon (measure 23) with a 3:2 ratio and
   ♩ ♪♩   pattern

A solo soprano sings a melismatic phrase, starting in measure 13, with an upward leap of a minor sixth. The rest of the melodic contour of this phrase emphasizes the tritone and chromatic formula.

The concluding phrase of the couplet section begins on a fortissimo high G and descends with leaps of a fifth and augmented fourth. In measure 20 the tritone interval is echoed first, a half-step, and then a minor third lower. The section ends with a great ritardando and decrescendo.

The *Rechant* begins the next section at an intensity of double forte to be sung by three contraltos and three basses. Messiaen achieves an antiphonal effect with the entrance of three sopranos and three tenors (measure 25) singing a fifth higher. The melodic line here consists of a theme called "Chant d'amour I" ("Song of Love"), which occurred in Movement II of the *Turangalîla-symphonie* in which this theme is played slowly, sweetly, and tenderly. Here Messiaen has directed it to be performed "vividly, lively, and gaily."

Symmetrical rhythms provide Messiaen with another form of irregularity of rhythms. The very basic idea of change of the rhythms in each measure is fundamental to his music at this time. He compares them to elements in nature such as "the veins of leaves or butterflies' wings" in his *Conférence de Bruxelles* of 1958.[6]

Another form of irregularity that is related to ancient Greece as well as to this music is that of heterogeneous measures. The term here refers to measures that involve modulation of rhythm such as from cretic to tribrach, from spondée to trochée, from antibacchic peon to spondée, all of which are evident in this music. This rhythmic modulation, or rhythmic metabola, is a basic principle for Messiaen.

The "Chant d'amour I" theme, which is now the melodic theme of the *Rechant,* sung in pseudo-Hindi, repeats (measures 27 through 31) at a dynamic level of double forte; the entire couplet is then reiterated. With reprise of the couplet, the melodic phrasing and rhythm are exactly the same, although the rhythm appears quite different. This time it is written in fourth notation; that is, in a normal meter now, even though the rhythm has a more natural relation to the irregular conception given in the first couplet.

A new contrast is provided by the spoken voices of the second and third tenors and basses chanting in pseudo-Hindi. The reason for the new

Example 37. *Cinq rechants,* No. 2, measures 32–38

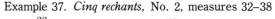

Extract from *Cinq rechants,* II, reproduced with permission. Copyright by Editions Salabert, Paris, France.

rhythmic notation is apparent. Another rhythmic pattern, added in the spoken voices, must be gathered into normal measures along with the original rhythmic pattern, which had contained great irregularity. By using the "false" notation, counter to the natural accents of the musical lines, the performance in ensemble becomes much more feasible.

In the tenor voice the rhythmic pattern consists of three Çârngadeva rhythms: râgavardhana, No. 93; candrakalâ, No. 105; and lackskmiça, No. 88. These three patterns, appeared in "Liturgie de cristal" (chapt. 7) in the form of a tâla or composite rhythm pattern, which is very significant in Messiaen's music.

The tâla rhythm is repeated twice in the tenor part throughout this couplet. Spoken by the second and third tenors in pseudo-Hindi, it provides an accompaniment to the contralto solo and other subsequent voicings. Brackets indicate the beginning and ending of the pattern. At the end of the couplet (measure 46) the tâla pattern breaks off, just slightly after the third pattern has begun.

The second and third basses also have an accompanying line spoken in pseudo-Hindi (see Example 37). The rhythm pattern in this line is the retrograde of the aforementioned tâla pattern in the tenor. The word syllables follow a normal order. The retrograde pattern is rather difficult to ascertain unless examined carefully, because the rests surrounding notes combine with note value in many cases to form the note durations of the Indian rhythms. The bass line tâla retrograde pattern is repeated twice and is also truncated after two more measures (measure 46).

The *Rechant* (measures 47 through 55) reiterates thematic material of the "Chant d'amour I" from Movement II of the *Turangalîla-symphonie* and then leads into a brief coda.

At the coda (measures 56 through 62) the first three bars of the tâla (tenor voice) and its retrograde (bass voice) repeats with the pseudo-Hindi chant spoken in a double pianissimo. Then, in measures 59 through 62, beginning at medium forte intensity, the final line of the melody with French text from the couplet returns once more, with the dynamics fading within the four bars to a triple pianissimo. The predominant intervals in this final line are the tritone and the minor second.

Although Messiaen continues to rely on chromatic formulas and the tritone, he is gradually moving toward tonal chromaticism. *Cinq rechants* also marks the end of a period where he makes extensive use of symbolism and surrealistic techniques. Combining text with spoken syllables and invented language, he created a work, a song of love, that allows complete abandon. The development of his rhythmic processes provides Messiaen with the freedom to achieve the effects he chooses. He uses rhythmic patterns from the one hundred twenty decî-tâla of Çârngadeva in rhythmic pedal and in retrograde. The added value rhythmic style is evident, as are non-retrogradable patterns. Messiaen's use of Greek meter, the primary unit of rhythm *(chronos protos),* and principles of irregularity are also apparent in the second *Rechant.*

Messiaen is already moving in the direction of rhythmic chromaticism with his use of the primary unit of rhythm. His involvement with superimposition of rhythms is beginning to decrease as he becomes more concerned with rhythmic manipulation.

10

Le livre d'orgue (1951)

During the next two decades Messiaen received increasing recognition. His success, although mixed with controversy, was apparent not only in his own country but throughout the world. He was becoming well known internationally as an interpreter of his own works; as a lecturer, new vistas were also opening.

Messiaen was receiving many illustrious invitations to speak in countries all over Europe as well as in the United States. In the summer of 1949 he traveled to the United States for the first time, where he was invited to teach composition at the Berkshire Music Center in Tanglewood. Other appearances and tours included Italy, Budapest, Darmstadt, and Sarrebrück.

Messiaen's personal life during these years was difficult. The serious illness of his first wife continued to cause tremendous stress and unhappiness, although during the 1940s he was able to release his torment through the composing of some of his best works. By the 1950s he was becoming increasingly drained by the never-ending strain caused by such an illness.

One continuing area of professional and personal satisfaction was found in his class at the Conservatory. Messiaen called forth feelings of tremendous loyalty and respect from his composition students, most of whom have continued to pay homage to him over the years. Pierre Boulez has described the "experience Messiaen" with high praise, stating that "only Messiaen's class could create among its students such conspiracy and togetherness, out of which grew the enthusiasm for new discoveries, for dissecting things and putting them through the mill."[1]

Boulez's experience, along with that of other students, represented the friendship and solidarity of a small group around a master who has unsettled and upset the critics.

Karlheinz Stockhausen, in a tribute to Messiaen, praised the teacher for encouraging his students to find their own way, and never trying to convince them to adopt his own practices, even when they pursued contrary methods, as did Stockhausen. He showed his students how he himself worked; he also showed his understanding of the music of others. For these brilliant pupils involved with forming the music of the future, Messiaen was the ideal teacher.

In 1949 Messiaen wrote a piano piece, "Mode de valeurs et d'intensitiés," from *Quatre études de rhythm,* which he intended as an experiment. Here was a piece of strict organization that determined the notes of the scale, the length of notes, the type of attack with which they were played, and their loudness. Messiaen had created the series of timbres, of rhythms and of intensities that he had contemplated for some time.

The following year he played a newly released recording of the piece for his students. Several of them insisted on playing the record at least twenty times. Messiaen's experiment had caught their total attention. Over and over they exclaimed that here at last was the first complete and methodical exploration of the universe of sound. One of these students who believed that Messiaen had revealed the secrets of a long-cherished dream was none other than Karlheinz Stockhausen.

The method of composition wherein the composer indicates the exact duration of each note as well as the exact intensity of each tone is a form of serialism that goes beyond the earlier twelve-note principle of Schoenberg. Whereas Schoenberg controlled the order of tones, Messiaen also controlled their duration, timbre, and intensity.

Other works written during this experimental period include *Cantéyodjavâ* for piano (1949), *Mess de la Pentecôte* for organ (1950), and *Livre d'orgue* (1951) for organ. All of these works contain various elements of the modal and rhythmic innovations developed during this time.

Le livre d'orgue, the last of his experimental works, explored Indian rhythms combined with serial procedures that are applied to pitch and rhythm. It is at the highest peak of Messiaen's rhythmic achievement. The first performance was at Stuttgart, Germany, in 1953; Messiaen performed the French premiere at la Sainte Trinité Church on March 21, 1955. Nearly two thousand people mobbed him as he tried to enter the church for that performance. By evening people had spread word throughout Paris that Olivier Messiaen was one of the greatest organists of the time, commending as well his brilliant contribution as composer.

Divided into seven movements, the work is extremely technical, severe in style, and cerebral in approach. Its analysis demands extreme patience and detail of explanation. The first movement, selected for analysis here, illustrates techniques that are basic to the understanding of future compositions. When one understands Messiaen's approach in the use of permutation and interversion, the addition of superimposed techniques is easier to assimilate.

Messiaen has arranged the seven movements in an order that produces a certain musical symmetry: movements I and VII are concerned with Indian rhythms and specific compositional devices; Movements II and VI are connected by the same pitch series; Movements III and V are similarly connected; while Movement IV provides the centerpiece of the work and uses birdsong.

Movement I, "Reprises par interversion" (meaning "repetition through reversal") is a monodic movement that divides into four sections. All of the musical material occurs in the first section. Sections II and III repeat the material by reversals or interversions, which explains the title of this movement. The rhythm of section I consists entirely of three Hindu rhythms:

P—pratâpaçekhara

G—gajahampa

S—sârasa

Each rhythm is one measure in length; the entire first section consists of eighteen measures. This allows the three rhythms to be presented in the six possible permutations. To illustrate, the rhythms are now referred to by initial:

Measures	1, 2, 3:	P G S
Measures	4, 5, 6:	P S G
Measures	7, 8, 9:	G S P
Measures	10, 11, 12:	G P S
Measures	13, 14, 15:	S G P
Measures	16, 17, 18:	S P G

One can see that permutations in Messiaen's work are types of symmetrical changes of a given series or row of numbers. He creates them by selecting a series of numbers, symbols, or rhythms (as in this case), and then arranges the rows so as to indicate a specific order of change for the subsequent permutations. Messiaen usually calls each individual series of reversals an interversion. Interversion, therefore, is the manner of manipulating a series by an ordered means of reversal, which we will illustrate further in sections I, II, III, and IV of "Reprises par interversion."

The Hindu rhythms that have been introduced are not only reordered by interversion, but are treated as rhythmic personages. (See chapt. 1, subheading Stravinsky.)

Pratâpaçekhara increases in value by a thirty-second note at each repetition; gajahampa begins in an augmented form and diminishes by a thirty-second note at each repetition; sârasa does not change. To Messiaen the rhythms represent various characters on the stage: the one in augmentation, the character who attacks; the one in diminution, the person attacked; the unchanging one, the motionless person. Therefore with each new appearance of the rhythm P, every note value is augmented by a thirty-second note:

P rhythm: (measure 1)

P¹ rhythm: (measure 4)

P² rhythm: (measure 9)

The gajahampa rhythm ♩ ♪ ♪ ♪♩ diminishes in value by a thirty-second note at each repetition, following Messiaen's practice of diminution. The sârasa rhythm remains unchanged.

In Example 38 are the first five measures of section I. Measures 1 through 3 show the original rhythm pattern of P, G, and S labeled in the score. Measures 4 and 5 illustrate the first rearrangement of the order of rhythms to P and S. The First series of twelve tones appear in measures 1 through 3, indicated by numbers 1 through 12. Directions of the dynamic levels and organ manuals for each rhythm pattern also appear in the score. In measure 4, the first repetition of P, each note value is augmented by a thirty-second note. The S pattern is measure 5 remains the same.

The directions for the dynamics and organ manuals follow a mode of dynamics and a mode of timbres Messiaen has devised:

P rhythm is always played on the Récit (upper manual or
    Choir), at a dynamic level of *mf.*

Example 38. *Le livre d'orgue,* "Reprises par interversion," section I, measures
1–5

Extract from *Le livre d'orgue* by Olivier Messiaen. Copyright by Alphonse Leduc & Cie.,
Paris, France.

> G rhythm is always played on the Positif (middle manual or
> Swell), at a dynamic level of *f,* and on the Pedal at a
> dynamic level of *ff.*

> S rhythm is always played on the Great (lower manual) at a
> level of *p.*

The terms Récit, Positif, and Great are French descriptions of the manuals, used here because the musical score identifies them in this way.

Each group of three rhythms uses a tone row of twelve pitches played on
three staves, with no pitch being repeated before the twelve tones have
been played. In section I Messiaen uses a total of six series of twelve
tones, which are reordered in later sections of the movement.

The first section of eighteen measures, containing the six possible
permutations, provides the basis for the remaining music of this movement. It is evident that after establishing the order of permutations and the
criteria for modes of timbre and dynamics, very little is left to choice
except for the order of pitches in each series of twelve tones. The
performer must have utmost control and technique to be able to execute
the rhythmic patterns according to the precise set values and dynamics.

Section II begins in measure 20, after a one-measure rest between
sections. The music of section II is a repetition through reversal of the
notes and rhythms of section I, which combines the music of the first half in
retrograde. By playing from the beginning and the end simultaneously the

music concludes in the middle. Section II contains nine measures:

⌊1 18⌋ ⌊2 17⌋ ⌊3 16⌋ ⌊4 15⌋ ⌊5 14⌋ ⌊6 13⌋ ⌊7 12⌋ ⌊8 11⌋ ⌊9 10⌋
   1   2   3   4   5   6   7   8   9

Messiaen has descibed this process as permutation in the form of a closed fan because of the progression inward (measures 1 and 18) from the ends to the middle of the music (measures 9 and 10).

Example 39. *Le livre d'orgue,* "Reprises par interversion," section I, measures 16–19

Extract from *Le livre d'orgue* by Olivier Messiaen. Copyright by Alphonse Leduc & Cie., Paris, France.

In Example 39, measures 16 through 18 show the last four bars of section I with the last (sixth) series of twelve tones and the three bars of Hindu rhythms in their final (sixth) stage of alteration. The rhythms P, G, and S appear in the sixth interversion as S, P, and G. The sârasa rhythm pattern remains unchanged. The P (measure 17) has been augmented by a thirty-second note in five repetitions; G (measure 18) has been diminished by a thirty-second note with each repetition (five). The final notes of the first section are numbered (61 through 72) to show the last series of pitches and corresponding rhythmic values. In section II the music of section I combines from ends to middle, distributing the numbered notes in alternation.

Example 40 shows the beginning of section II. In measure 20 are the notes of measures 1 and 18 of section I.

Measure 21 contains the notes of measures 2 and 17 of section I. The notes of the first series (numbered 1 through 12) appear in normal order; notes of the sixth series (numbered 61 through 72) appear in retrograde. In

Example 40. *Le livre d'orgue,* "Reprises par interversion," section II, measures 20–21

Extract from *Le livre d'orgue* by Olivier Messiaen. Copyright by Alphonse Leduc & Cie., Paris, France.

measure 20 the notes of rhythm P (first series) combine with notes of rhythm G (diminution[5]); measure 21 contains notes of G and notes of pattern P (augmented[5]). This reordering of the notes and rhythms continues with each measure, ending with measures 9 and 10 of section I (middle of the section).

The organ manuals assigned originally to each rhythm pattern remain the same, so that in each measure there are now rapid changes to different manuals. The effect is kaleidoscopic; the original forms are fragmented and scattered. Messiaen describes this process as "the rhythmic personnages are decapitated, dismembered, 'proteiforme' monster which climbs to the arm of this one, to the hand of that one, to the perfume of this one, to the color of that one."[2]

Section III is produced by the reversal of the process of section II. It combines the retrograde of the first half of section I with the normal order of the second half. Again, it encompasses nine measures rather than the original eighteen.

⌊10 9⌋ ⌊11 8⌋ ⌊12 7⌋ ⌊13 6⌋ ⌊14 5⌋ ⌊15 4⌋ ⌊16 3⌋ ⌊17 2⌋ ⌊18 1⌋
  1   2   3   4   5   6   7

This type of permutation Messiaen describes as an open fan because it gives the impression of opening from the center to the outer ends. This entire section can also be considered the retrograde of section II if one compares the numerical order of measures as indicated above.

Section IV is the complete retrograde of section I. We have therefore a piece that divides in half; the second half a retrograde of the first.

Figure 2. General form of *Le livre d'orgue,* "Reprises par inter-version"

Section I	Section II	Section III	Section IV
measures 1–19	measures 20–29	measures 30–39, retrograde section II	measures 40–57, retrograde section I

Le livre d'orgue is at the highest peak of Messiaen's rhythmic achievements. With its highly ordered structure it is a tour de force. Using Hindu rhythms and the procedure of rhythmic personnages, Messiaen developed the techniques of interversion and permutation to a high level of complexity. In "Reprises par interversion" he included techniques of augmentation (pratâpacekhara) and diminution (gajahampa). He used new modes such as those introduced in *Mode de valeurs et d'intensitiés. Le livre d'orgue,* in addition to the six series of twelve pitches, contains a mode of timbres and of intensities.

The techniques developed by Messiaen during the experimental period opened up whole new areas of exploration for the avant-garde composers of the twentieth century. Many have pursued the possibilites further than Messiaen himself cared to do; however, facets of these innovations occur in varying degrees of complexity in nearly all of Messiaen's subsequent works. He developed serial procedures in the *Catalogue d'oiseaux* (Chapt. 12); the technique of permutation is an important feature in *Le merle noir* (Chapt. 11). After *Le livre d'orgue* Messiaen turned from the strictly structured writing style to nature and concentrated exclusively on birdsong for his inspiration. We examine works so inspired in the last two chapters.

11

Le merle noir (1951)

With Messiaen's ever-growing international fame have come continual demands on his time. Although he has tried to meet these demands with patience and courtesy, he dislikes any intrusion into his private life. Perhaps this desire to retire from the public eye began with the illness of his first wife. Very likely the attacks by critics on works composed during the 1940s added new scars. The works that drew their inspiration from the Tristan myth were about a supreme passionate love that remains unconsummated and finds fulfillment only in death. Messiaen's detractors have continually attempted to show that such indications of a highly passionate temperament are incongruous in one who claims to have such strong religious convictions.

While most of Messiaen's students remained loyal, there were a few who had left him to experience other avant-garde disciplines. It was not until the period of Messiaen's experiments with total organization that all of his students united in his support, declaring the vital contributions that had been made by the master in the realms of rhythm.

The discoveries he made during the experimental period provided him with continued recognition, however; not only by the public, who already loved his music, but by peers, fellow composers, and critics. Messiaen himself did not extend his probings into the limitless possibilities opened up by total organization. At the very time that students and other composers began to explore these possibilities further, Messiaen retreated into nature and began in earnest to develop his techniques for transferring the songs of birds to music paper. Perhaps this was a retreat from the world and some of its inhabitants who had caused him pain. Possibly it was a choice he made concerning something he had always wanted to explore.

Messiaen considers birds to be "our desire for light, for the stars, for rainbows and jubilant song." By the end of 1953, their songs occupied an almost exclusive place in his works.

Messiaen made use of birdsong in two different ways: by treating it as malleable material and by trying to illustrate the most exact musical portrait possible. Among the shorter works that followed the composition of the Tristan trilogy, *Le merle noir* is particularly significant because it illustrates successfully the transition from the experimentation to Messiaen's exclusive focus on birdsong. Composed near the end of the experimental years (1949–1951), it reflects some of the developments in his techniques at that time and also anticipates compositional techniques of the larger bird pieces written in the later 1950s, such as *Catalogue d'oiseaux,* which attempts to evoke the bird's habitat and the atmosphere surrounding it.

The song of the blackbird, melodic in style, has many patterns as is evident in this short piece for flute and piano. From the first flute cadenza in the introduction, one discovers specific characteristics of the blackbird's song. Later in the piece the song appears once more in solo; but just as the text might change in an art song, the content of the birdsong varies melodically while still containing characteristic intervallic relationships. The blackbird *Turdus merula* in Latin, appears in several subsequent larger works by Messiaen: *Reveil des oiseaux, Catalogue d'oiseaux, Chronochromie, Le transfiguration,* and *Meditation sur la mystère de la Saint Trinité.*

During the experimental period Messiaen introduced and developed the techniques of employing series of timbres, intensities, and durations (we discuss this procedure more fully in the section on "La chouette hulotte," chapt. 12). Another technique from the same period was that of permutation. Drew says regarding this device of Messiaen's:

An interest in permutation is as natural a consequence of Messiaen's desire to destroy traditional thematicism as his attitude to chromaticism is a consequence of his desire to overthrow traditional tonality.[1]

Le merle noir illustrates this compositional device quite clearly, because the time-value series, being limited to four durations, is more easily comprehensible than some other more complex works.

The outer structural form of this piece is clearly discernible through examination of variations of birdsong and through the interrelationship of piano and flute material. The piano provides musical contrast; as the piece progresses it also indicates conversation between two birds (flute and piano) that later becomes a very animated, excited "discussion" at the coda. There is definitely a sense of thematic repetition reinforced by the call and response between the instruments. One must look at factors of timbre and texture as well, in the grouping of material, to determine the symmetry and form of the work as a whole.

Viewed from this perspective, the piece is a binary form, outlined as follows:

Formal outline of *Le merle noir*

Section *A*—flute solo (blackbird)	(measures 1–8)
Section *B*	
a—theme	(measures 9–26)
b—commentary	(measures 27–35)
transition	(measures 36–43)
Section *A'*—flute solo	(measures 44–53)
Section *B'*	
a'—theme in canonic form	(measures 54–71)
b'—commentary	(measures 72–82)
transition	(measures 83–90)
Coda—permutations	(measures 91–125)

In the introduction (measures 1 through 8) there is a rush of notes using chromatic half-steps in the bass register of the piano. This is sustained for a duration of three bars, and establishes a mood of mystery prior to the entrance of the solo birdsong depicted by the flute with a wide range of notes as well as abrupt changes in intensity from *ff* to *ppp*. Messiaen reproduces faithfully the contours and the melodic configurations of the blackbird's song. His process of doing so, briefly discussed in chapter 1, involves only the necessary modifications in adapting the song to the musical instruments.

The rhythmic patterns also derive from nature, although in some cases they are somewhat slower if the original song is very quick. Messiaen has stated in *Technique* that birdsong does not fit into his four classifications of notation.[2] He notates the measures with barlines according to the phrasing of the song, which is usually very irregular. Messiaen uses no time signature; rhythmic patterns adhere to strict time values, using the short or primary note value *(chronos protos)* and its free multiplication in the manner of ancient Greeks.

In using the primary note value here, Messiaen expresses the ratio of values with added fractions in some measures (e.g., 2:1½, first part of measure 7). This type of measure is irrational, as opposed to rational measures that are expressed entirely by integral numbers.

Iwanka Krastewa mentions the principle of irrational measures as one of the procedures in Messiaen's practice that is also related to ancient Greek metrics:

The theory of Aristoxenes also involves measures which have irrational lengths which can only be expressed by fractions of the primary beat. Whereas rational measures (having simple, double or hemiola ratios) are expressed by integral numbers (1:1, 2:1, 3:2), irrational measures must be expressed by ratios of 2:1½, 3:2½, et cetera.[3]

In writing birdsong, it is obvious that this is a case of related principles rather than of copying of procedures. Both rational and irrational measures can be present in an irregular rhythmic expression, which is the desired mode of expression in all of Messiaen's music. Reproduction of the patterns of birdsong certainly strengthen his argument that the irregular or ametrical music is most akin to nature.

The flute solo contains all twelve tones, although it is not serial. Messiaen uses different arrangements of the predominant intervals (e.g., the tritone): utilizing added notes to vary the phrase, or transposing a phrase up a major third to keep the same melodic shape. In addition to the tritone, which appears frequently, the appoggiatura is heard, as is the trill. Change of register, interspersed rests, and rapid changes of intensity are other factors that create a very realistic facsimile of the song of a bird. Example 41 illustrates the first six measures of *Le merle noir*. Brackets indicate the predominant tritone interval. As section *A* ends, the flute solo plays the same flurry of chromatic notes with which the piano began the section.

At section *B*, measures 9 through 11 (Example 42), the thematic material begins in the piano with an exact response from the flute in measures 12 through 14. Although most of the piece is in the twelve-tone mode, the first thematic melody line of section *B* belongs to mode 7, sixth transposition, the most chromatic of Messiaen's modes of limited transposition. The left hand of the piano theme is composed entirely of the tritone interval, which moves chromatically. All twelve tones are used in this passage.

The second phrase, introduced in the piano, is a cyclic theme from *Turangalîla-symphonie*, the "Chant d'amour I," already heard in *Cinq*

Example 41. *Le merle noir,* section *A,* measures 1–6

Extract from *Le merle noir* by Olivier Messiaen. Copyright by Alphonse Leduc & Cie., Paris, France.

Example 42. *Le merle noir,* section *B,* measures 9–12

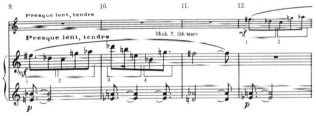

Extract from *Le merle noir* by Olivier Messiaen. Copyright by Alphonse Leduc & Cie., Paris, France.

Example 43. *Le merle noir,* section *B,* measures 23–26

Extract from *Le merle noir* by Olivier Messiaen. Copyright by Alphonse Leduc & Cie., Paris, France.

rechants. The flute repeats this phrase (measures 19 through 22). The flute then states a phrase of its own in a descending passage (measures 23 through 26), which forms the consequent phrase of the theme and provides a cadence effect. Expansion of the last note (measure 26) also provides the feeling of a cadence. In this descending phrase, the significant intervallic leap is that of a minor ninth (D-flat to D) (see Example 43). This consequent phrase is in mode 3, first transposition.

In section *B,* Greek rhythmic patterns appear. (The pattern is identified by a dot signifying short duration; the dash indicates a long duration.) These patterns may be seen in the measures of Example 43 according to the numbered brackets.

1. Trochée   (- .)

2. Tribrach   (. . .)

3. Cretic   (- . -)

4. Iambic   (. -)

5. Anapest   (. . -)

6. Antibacchic   (- - .)

Of these rhythms, three occur in this passage as so-called irrational patterns. For example, the trochée occurred first in this piece with the pattern of ♩ ♪   ; then in measure 9 the pattern becomes ♪ ♪   . The interrelationship of the two is the same (- .), but one unit in the second pattern is smaller. Two other rhythmic patterns that are treated as irrational values in theme *a* are the iambic (measures 10 and 13) and the anapest (measure 21).

Some of the rhythms identified as Greek patterns are similar to Gregorian neumes; the Latin equivalent for the Greek iamb pattern (♪ ♩) would be the *podatus* (Latin name). The Latin equivalent for the cretic rhythm in Greece, ♫♩ (measure 10), is *porrectus;* while the anapest, ♫♩   , has its Latin equivalent in the neume *scandicus,* which would be transcribed in the same way.

In Example 43, measures 25 and 26, notice the bracketed rhythm (No. 4) iamb, which is repeated with inexact augmentation in order to slow for closing of the phrase. In the left hand, the four chord changes are progressively lengthened by inexact augmentation, combining the dot and added or increased note values.

The second section of *B* begins the commentary (measure 27). The first two measures consist of a series of leaps ranging from diminished fourths to major ninths. The leaps are a condensation of much of the intervallic usage in the theme; this is the fragmentary material to be developed as commentary on the theme.

The flute exactly duplicates the first phrase; it is accompanied by chords that use a wide range and three staves on the piano. The use of harmony with birdsong is mainly to provide harmonic resonance and thus reproduce more exactly the correct timbre. Messiaen discussed the problem of achieving accurate timbre effect in birdsong[4]; this continued to be his main concern throughout the writing of *Catalogue d'oiseaux* (1958).

In this work, due to the writing of the composer and the execution of the performer, the timbre and texture of the two instruments blend in a very natural way. The chromatic chords in the piano that follow in the commentary section (measures 30 through 34) duplicate the flute line, providing added resonance. This sequence of chords belongs to mode 7; in their pattern of descent they pass through fourth, fifth, third, and second transpositions. The flute line belongs to third transposition.

The music moves in measures 36 through 43 with a flurry of material that contains intervallic leaps, arpeggios, and appoggiaturas surrounding the trills on D. This rapidly moving passage has a transitional function that leads once more to the solo cadenza of the flute (measures 44 through 53).

The material of section *A'* is another paraphrase of the blackbird's song that Messiaen has reproduced as accurately as possible. The melody has characteristics indicating the similarity to the first appearance, but it is basically new. Because of the essentially nonrepetitive nature of birdsong, thematic processes along traditional lines are not suitable.

The melody also includes inversions of intervals, transpositions of intervals, ascending appoggiaturas, and more abrupt contrast in dynamics. The chromatic passage that concluded the opening melody with ascending motion now returns at the end; but it now has a descending line, indicating a closing of the solo.

Theme *a'* returns now in measures 54 through 71, repeating the exact melodic notes as well as the rhythm of the first occurrence in *a*.

Although the rhythmic values are the same, this theme has different notation in the flute part. The purpose is to accommodate the canonic imitation, with the flute part entering at a distance of ten sixteenth notes (see Example 44).

Example 44. *Le merle noir,* section *B'*, measures 54–57

Extract from *Le merle noir* by Olivier Messiaen. Copyright by Alphonse Leduc & Cie., Paris, France.

The tritone accompaniment in the piano, left hand, is still evident although the pattern changes slightly (first two intervals reversed) along with the rhythmic values. The rhythm pattern, however, does not vary according to a unified plan of augmentation or diminution.

The beginning of section *b'* is more a continuing part of the previous section than its counterpart in section *b* (measure 27) because of the continued canonic imitation. Measures 75 through 82 of the commentary once more echo a passage from the previous material in *b*. The modal chords (mode 7) return with a few differences, such as the interversion of some measures (e.g., measures 77 and 78 are now the reverse of measures 31 and 32). There is also octave displacement and extension of the passage by repetition. Messiaen transposes the last two measures of the commentary up a fourth from the original, causing the subsequent transitional material to be repeated a fourth higher also. This second part of the binary form gives the effect of the conversation of two birds; the piano blending effectively with the flute while aided by the canon form.

Arriving at the coda, the remainder of the piece involves the technique of permutation (measures 91 through 125), which we will redefine briefly.

Permutation and interversion are terms that Messiaen sometimes uses interchangeably. One notes that he used the term interversion in his early periods to discuss the practice of changing the order of notes. The term also could mean, simply, inversion or transposition of notes. Later, when Messiaen began manipulating rhythmic values, he used the term permutation. Interversion is usually the term he uses when the work involves manipulation by a given series such as retrograde, ends to center, center to ends, and so on. He often identifies the plan of manipulation in a score or the preface to the score.

Permutation means the exchange of order, or the manipulation of a group or series of chromatic rhythms. By chromatic rhythm is meant a series of note values that move progressively to the next larger or smaller value, using the primary note value.

With the sixteenth note as the *chronos protos,* the chromatic series in *Le merle noir* is as follows:

In the top line of the piano part, measure 91, is the first permutation, which happens to be the order of the chromatic series (see Example 45). Next Messiaen uses all of these values in varying order for successive passages until he has completed 24 patterns. The bottom staff of the piano

Example 45. *Le merle noir,* coda, measures 91–94

Extract from *Le merle noir* by Olivier Messiaen. Copyright by Alphonse Leduc & Cie., Paris, France.

follows its own order of permutation, using the same series of four-note values. It is probably easier to examine one line and its permutations at a time; so the order has been illustrated with the upper staff of the piano first, as follows:

Permutation	*Series*
1	1 2 3 4
2	1 2 4 3
3	1 3 2 4
4	1 3 4 2
5	1 4 3 2
6	1 4 2 3
7	3 4 1 2
8	3 4 2 1
9	3 1 2 4
10	3 1 4 2
11	3 2 4 1
12	3 2 1 4
13	2 1 3 4
14	2 1 4 3
15	2 3 4 1
16	2 3 1 4
17	2 4 3 1
18	2 4 1 3
19	4 1 2 3
20	4 1 3 2
21	4 2 1 3
22	4 2 3 1
23	4 3 2 1
24	4 3 1 2

Each permutation of the series is marked in brackets in both lines of Example 45, extending through three of the permutations.

On can see by examining the order of the twenty-four permutations that Messiaen uses all the possible combinations beginning with the number 1, through the first six permutations. Then beginning with the number 3, he again follows through the possible permutations in order. There are six different series for every number, making a total of 24.

In the bottom line the pattern is slightly different:

Permutation	Series
1	2 1 3 4
2	2 1 4 3
3	2 3 4 1
4	2 3 1 4
5	2 4 3 1
6	2 4 1 3
7	4 1 2 3
8	4 1 3 2
9	4 2 1 3
10	4 2 3 1
11	4 3 2 1
12	4 3 1 2
13	1 2 3 4
14	1 2 4 3
15	1 3 2 4
16	1 3 4 2
17	1 4 3 2
18	1 4 2 3
19	3 4 1 2
20	3 4 2 1
21	3 1 2 4
22	3 1 4 2
23	3 2 4 1
24	3 2 1 4

In examining the first column of numbers in both series, it is apparent that Messiaen has arranged the order so that no rhythmic value occurs simultaneously at the beginning of each series. As the upper staff explores the possibilities for rhythmic value 1, the lower staff completes the possible permutations for rhythmic value 2, and so forth throughout the order of numbers.

At this point, the "song" material in the flute part consists of particularly repetitive staccato patterns that resembles a rhythmic pedal. The intervals reverse occasionally and the appoggiaturas become more frequent as the intervallic pattern continues its contour of leaps through fourths, fifths, sixths, and sevenths. The total effect is that of animated chatter, which is scarcely distinguishable from the piano with its separate patterns of varied rhythms. Thus the entire picture might be the conversation of three birds in chorus, with each making his own statement.

The "conversation" ends abruptly in the piano, measure 120, with an upward sweep of the piano lines as the flute completes a winding, descending curve. The piece does not fade away, but completes the coda with three resonating chords that encompass all registers of the piano at double forte intensity. The flute plays a final brief arc of six notes in the top register at double forte with a final appoggiatura sixteenth note that is accented with *fff* intensity.

Le merle noir is an excellent short work that demonstrates the use of birdsong's melodic contour as the principal musical material. It briefly uses thematic material from Messiaen's Tristan trilogy, but most of the music is from the twelve-tone mode, patterned after the melodic contour of the song of the blackbird. Irrational measures and values, Greek rhythms, and inexact augmentation occur and convey more naturally the reproduction of the birdsong and its precise but irregular rhythms. Messiaen has used a characteristic device in writing a rhythmic and melodic canon in *Le merle noir* for the piano and flute. The manipulation of rhythms has become a major feature rather than the superimposition of layers of rhythms. Messiaen's use of permutation in *Le merle noir* vividly illustrates this process.

12

Catalogue d'oiseaux (1958)

Olivier Messiaen took seriously his great love for birds and their songs. His first attempts to notate the songs went very badly, according to him; he had no idea of which birds were singing. Deeply mortified by his ignorance, he sought the advice of some professional ornithologists. From that time on, he has studied with a series of four or five experts in France, going with them to various estates and regions of his country to learn more about birds. As he continued to study and notate the songs of different species his collection grew quite impressive. Eventually he was able to recognize by ear and without hesitation the songs of fifty species in France. There are approximately five hundred and fifty other species living in France and Europe that Messiaen can recognize after a moment's reflection or after looking at them with binoculars. He also knows well some of the birds of North America and many of Japan, having studied them while on tour. As each species has its own recognizable song, Messiaen became more and more immersed in reproducing these songs so that recognizable portraits could be presented.

Each species expresses several intentions by their songs or by calls, as the professional ornithologists classify their sounds. The songs of birds express the affirmation of their own territory, their amorous or courting impulse, and, most beautiful of all, their salutes to the dawning or dying light. The songs are a true musical language wherein precise meanings are conveyed and through which birds are enabled to communicate with their society.

Messiaen has been more willing to elaborate in interviews on the songs of birds than any other topic. When engaged in a dialogue on the subject, his tremendous knowledge is evident. He is familiar not only with the calls of many species, but with the variety of repertoire in song that a bird acquires throughout his lifetime.

The domain of birdsong seems to belong exclusively to Messiaen. He is quite aware that none of his students has followed him in this pursuit. Whereas his advances in the rhythmic studies served as a springboard for discoveries of his contemporaries, Messiaen pursued his work among the birds quite alone.

Messiaen has written the songs of birds using two different methods. In one he treats the songs as malleable material, creating many kinds of manipulations in the manner of electronic music. In his larger works, such as *Catalogue d'oiseaux,* he tries to outline the most exact musical portrait possible. With this method the composer tries to depict exactly the song of a typical bird of a district, surrounded by its neighbors. He also endeavors to indicate the singing at different hours of the day and night, while presenting in the harmonic and rhythmic material the colors of the landscape in which the bird lives.

Although Messiaen realizes that other people may not agree as to the exactitude of what he portrays in a given landscape or portrait, he is quite proud of the authentic results he has achieved. His intention has been for the listener, who might know a particular bird or landscape, to receive special pleasure of rediscovery by the recognition they find through Messiaen's music.

His desire to translate nature into musical terms stems from his feeling that nature is the most perfect reality in our world. Messiaen has stated that "among the artistic hierarchy, the birds are probably the greatest musicians to inhabit our planet."[1]

Catalogue d'oiseaux is the most important work of this period. Messiaen represents musically not only the various birds, but different aspects of nature, including mountains, rivers, the sea, cliffs, flowers, and sunrise. He has chosen the piano to represent the unique characteristics of the birds, because this instrument has a tremendous musical range and can give a wide variety of expression and intensity.

"La chouette hulotte," the seventh movement of *Catalogue d'oiseaux,* describes an aspect of the night that is sinister and terrifying. The title refers to the tawny owl, which is one of the several owls that inhabit Orgeval forests and who give their noctural calls after midnight.

Messiaen has described the tawny owl and its habitat in the notes to the recording of *Catalogue d'oiseaux:*

His plumage is spotted with brown and red, his mysterious wise face with the encircled eyes, looks supernaturally solemn, but his noctural voice is more capable of provoking terror than his appearance. I heard it often, around 2:00 a.m., in the Orgeval forests, St. Germain-en-Laye. . . .

Fearful, heartbeat-accelerating screech-owl yelps, cries of the long-eared owl, and the tawny owl calls: at once lugubrious and pained, vague and strangely disquieting, terrifyingly vociferous like a child being murdered! Silence. More faraway howls like bells from another world . . . [2]

The most significant reason for the choice of "La chouette hulotte" in this analytical work, beyond the interest in perceiving how Messiaen translates its picture into musical terms, is his combination of compositional techniques. Rather than using the modes of limited transposition, impressionistic techniques, or other earlier devices, this piece explores the most recent extension of Messiaen's musical language. The techniques involved in "La chouette hulotte" derive from his experimental period, which proved to be the starting point for the avant-garde that followed Messiaen and moved into areas of serial and electronic composition. This work evolves from the principles of an earlier work, "Mode de valeurs et d'intensités," which took musical constants of thirty-six notes, twenty-four note values, twelve types of attacks (accents), and seven dynamic levels. These constants divided into three series of twelve notes that were called modes. Each mode was on a separate staff, although the ranges overlapped; each note was assigned a dynamic level and type of attack. Messiaen arranged the notes of each group in such a way as to avoid sounding one at the same time as another part. This was the only time that Messiaen used a mode through an entire piece with such strict limitations.

In "La chouette hulotte" Messiaen makes use of his mode of values and intensities, but only in one section of the piece; therefore its characteristic color provides contrast with those of the other musical material. He has written the mode on three lines of the bass clef. He has eliminated the previous serialization of attacks; the mode here concerns only the factors of pitch, duration, and intensity (dynamic levels).

This procedure differs from a serial procedure in that the notes have been chosen freely from the group rather than following a fixed order. Instead of an order of notes fixed by the series, the characteristics of each note, that is, its duration and dynamics, established for a certain pitch remain fixed.

In organizing the material of "La Chouette hulotte" it is necesary to consider it in terms of the ideas or images that Messiaen presents. The general format of the movement consists of two couplets and two refrains. Within these larger sections are subsections that are determined not thematically, but rather by shape, texture, register, or similar characteristics. The subsections present ideas or images that range from human emotion to birdcalls to the setting of the habitat.

In this piece, Messiaen has specified in the score, the names of three varieties of owls that appear in the nocturnal setting. He uses the modified mode of pitches, durations and intensities, which are more fully explained later, to evoke the setting of night.

The setting of musical sounds of night opens the work and reoccurs approximately in the middle of the piece. In using the terms couplet and refrain, the form can be analyzed as section A and A', forming a refrain (night) to the couplets of section B and B' (a reversal of the usual order of terms). The couplets of section B contain subsections made up of two kinds of material: (1) birdsong, consisting of the short cries and calls of various species of the owl, and (2) non-birdsong material denoting the emotion of fear.

Messiaen acknowledges that he has written descriptive words in the score that indicate the human world in which birds live.[3] In other words, the fear depicted musically is the human emotion that the cry of the owl generates, and words descriptive of "La chouette hulotte" ("vague and terrifying") are human reactions to the owl's sounds.

In organizing the material of this piece, then, in terms of two refrains and two couplets, a basic binary form, $ABA'B'$ may be outlined in the following way:

Formal outline of "La Chouette Hulotte"

Section A	(measures 1–26)
Refrain—night	
Section B	(measures 27–63)
Couplet	
a—fear	(measures 27–32)
b—hibou moyen-duc	(measure 33)
(Long-eared owl)	
c—chouette cheveche	(measures 34–36)
(little owl)	
d—chouette hulotte	(measure 37)
(tawny owl)	
a'—fear	(measures 38–42)
b'—long-eared owl	(measures 43–49)
c'—little owl	(measures 50–52)
d'—tawny owl	(measures 53–63)
Section A'	(measures 64–118)
Refrain—night	

Section *B'* (measures 119–153)

   Couplet

      a^2—fear (measures 119–124)

      b^2—long-eared owl (measures 125–129)

      c^2—little owl (measures 130–131)

      b^3—long-eared owl (measures 132–133)

      c^3—little owl (measures 134–136)

      d^2—tawny owl (measures 137–153)

These units will now be examined in terms of texture, dynamics, mode, register, rhythmic characteristics, and tonal or atonal implications.

The pitches of section *A* derive from a mode that consists not only of pitches, but durations and intensities. The mode of pitches, durations, and intensities ranges from the A above middle C to the bottom B-flat on the piano, a span of four octaves in the middle and lower registers. Example 46 illustrates the first octave of the mode (in descending order), indicating the fixed duration and intensity that has been assigned to each pitch, starting from A above middle C.

Each of these notes has a fixed duration that progresses chromatically from the thirty-second note (A natural) as the notes descend chromatically. Each descending note is one thirty-second note longer than the preceding one; the lowest note (bottom A on the piano) consists of forty-nine thirty-second notes, or the equivalent of three tied half notes plus one thirty-second note.

The intensities, assigned in a chromatic order, descend from A to D-sharp *(ppp);* the intensity then increases as the descending scale continues, until it arrives once more at A (see Example 46). This arrangement results in each pitch, no matter what the octave, having the same intensity; that is, all As are marked *f;* F-sharps and Cs are marked *f;* Fs and C-sharps are marked *p;* Es and Ds are *pp;* and D-sharps have the intensity of *ppp* (see Example 46).

Example 46. Mode of pitches, duration, and intensities in "La chouette hulotte"

Example 47. *Catalogue d'oiseaux,* "La chouette hulotte," section *A,* "night," measures 1–21

Extract from *Catalogue d'oiseaux* by Olivier Messiaen. Copyright by Alphonse Leduc & Cie., Paris, France.

In the *A* section or refrain (measures 1 through 26), two bass staffs using all the pitches of the mode form a texture made up of three single lines or three-part polyphony (see Example 47).

It is clear that the notes in each line that forms the polyphony are not selected according to serial rules; nor do all twelve pitches occur before one in repeated. The first note of the mode (A above middle C) appears only once in this section (measure 8). The second note of the mode occurs in measure 4; the third (G) appears in measure 13 with the fixed duration and intensity established by the mode (see Examples 46 and 47). The first note, top staff of the section, is the fourth note in the modal series. The remaining notes of the three single lines, which may be located in this manner, are consistent with the fixed duration and intensity value established by the mode.

In the opening measures (measures 1 through 3) of section *A* the upper tetrachord of the F-sharp major scale descends in the top line (with octave displacement). Messiaen is obviously more concerned with creating an atmosphere than with melodic considerations, however. He has selected his notes to provide dynamic contrast as well as to create a balance of timbre within the polyphonic strands. The tritone appears regularly (measures 4, 8, 13, 17, and 22) and might be considered a unifying factor in the section. Harmonic and textural criteria are also considerations in the selection of notes; he consistently avoids repetition of notes in a vertical line.

The top line of the three-strand polyphony moves more rapidly than the other two lines because of the construction of the mode, with the shorter durations in the top octave. The contrast of the top line with the bottom line is apparent in Example 47. In addition to the difference of durations, Messiaen uses many angular, wide leaps in the top line, with very few intervals as small as a minor third. The bottom line moves chromatically or with stepwise motion; an interval of more than a tritone in this line is rare. The middle line of music expresses itself midway between the two contrasting outer lines. Its motion consists of small intervallic leaps, usually of a third, fourth, or fifth, with only occasional large leaps or stepwise motion. In the closing measures of section *A* (measures 23 through 25), the bottom line reverses the first two tones (F-sharp to F) in the first measure, top line of the piece.

At measure 27 the *B* section begins; it contains several short passages of different material. Unit *A*, designated by Messiaen as "fear" (measures 27 through 32), consists of six measures centered on low C in the bass clef, with one variant in the quick leap to the tritone (F-sharp). The use of rests groups the notes into short patterns. This monophonic line of repeated tones increases in intensity from *pp* to *mf* (see Example 48).

Example 48. *Catalogue d'oiseaux,* "La chouette hulotte," section *B,* "fear" measures 27–32

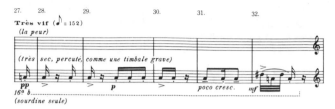

The music switches abruptly to the treble clef for the cry of the long-eared owl *b* in measure 33. This call is not a song in that the owl does not sing; rather, it is a brief pattern that is quite dissonant. The vertical harmony emphasizes intervals of sevenths, while ascending arpeggios use augmented octaves (e.g., B-flat and B) in the treble clef range. The tempo is quick; intensity is in the *mf* to *f* range, and the call breaks off abruptly with a decrease in this intensity to *p*. The brief passage is homophonic, consisting of two-part chords (see Example 49).

Example 49. *Catalogue d'oiseaux,* "La chouette hulotte," section *B,* measure 33

The next measure is the call of the little owl *c,* which contrasts sharply with the previous species of owl. Messiaen designates a mewing sound in the directions, along with a moderate tempo. This call, musically portrayed by two rapidly ascending scales combining pentatonic and the C major scales becomes increasingly faint as the line reaches the top. Messiaen has highlighted the minor third interval in this passage. The cry of the long-eared owl ends with three sharp, forte chords using seconds, directed to be performed as a yelp in the high register of the piano.

The tawny owl *d* appears briefly in measure 37 and indicates with two chords, the basic call, which is expanded in the next repetitions (see Example 50).

Example 50. *Catalogue d'oiseaux,* "La chouette hulotte," section *B,* measure 37

Extract from *Catalogue d'oiseaux* by Olivier Messiaen. Copyright by Alphonse Leduc & Cie., Paris, France.

The homophonic texture of this measure calls for varying levels of intensity within the chord. The pianist must play the outer tones softly, with two center tones C and A accented and marked forte. These two center tones suggest A minor, which is brought out in later repetitions of tawny owl.

These brief passages complete all the subsections that vary slightly in extension as they reappear.

In measure 38 the same monophonic line signifying fear returns with different rhythmic durations but the same span of intensities. The only change in the pattern of repeated C tones is the addition of an upper neighboring tone, D-flat. As the passage crescendos, the cry of the long-eared owl returns at measure 43, *b'*. Although dissonances are the same here as in the earlier section of the long eared owl, the texture has become thicker. This time the abrupt end is at an intensity of *ff,* with an upward intervallic leap of a major and a diminished seventh.

Theme *c* repeats the ascending runs of the little owl, with two sharply dissonant yelps in the high register of the piano (measures 50 through 52).

Once more the tawny owl returns in *d',* rendering more numerous calls in slow, sustained dissonances. Messiaen describes the first group as "mournful and sad." The repeated call continues to center on the notes of A and C. The clusters of tones formed by seconds surrounds the two tones as A moves to C and back, which gives the basic call of the owl the effect of added resonance.

The density increases in measure 56 with the addition of more dissonant tones. Again, varying intensities occur within a single chord. In measure

57 the sharply dissonant intervals repeat in a higher register of the piano at *fff* intensity; again the recurrence of the C to A interval in measure 58.

Messiaen continues the calls of the tawny owl "vague and terrifying" in measures 59 and 60, with movement of fifths reinforcing the A to C in the right hand, and with augmented octaves, first in the left hand and later in the right (measure 60).

The last passage of the tawny owl call in this couplet becomes suddenly quicker and quite soft; it consists of numerous repeated fifths in the left hand against the major seventh interval in the right. This movement continues rapidly, only to disappear suddenly into a long silence, signalling the ending of the first couplet.

The "night" refrain resumes in measures 64 through 118. This refrain is totally different in terms of arrangement of order of the pitches, although once more the pitches belong to the mode illustrated in Example 46. The first note of the mode (A above middle C) appears six times in this section, occurring the first time in the sixth measure (measure 69). The second note of the mode (G-sharp) does not appear until the seventh measure of the section (measure 70), as compared with measure 4 of the first refrain that began "La chouette hulotte." Once again the selection of notes from the mode is free; it is apparent that all twelve notes need not be sounded before any one tone is repeated. All the values, however, remain the same; the assigned durations and intensities remain fixed. Rather than repeating a symbolic mixture for night, indications of the continuing differences in its aspect appear as the night continues.

The bottom line begins with movements of small intervals, but after six measures the line begins a series of wide leaps (measure 70), which are then alternated with the smaller intervals. Only the first and last parts of the section are played 8va, or an octave lower (in the very bottom range of the piano).

On the other hand, the top line is much less angular, and combines smaller leaps with the very wide jumps used previously.

The result of these differences is a closer proximity of the three lines of music covering less of the outer extremities of the mode. Messiaen still selects the notes so as to provide constant change in the dynamics. Sudden contrasts in dynamics in a single line are frequent, yet the balance of contrast in pitches that form a vertical line is always constant.

At measure 109 the tones move an octave lower. The bottom two lines are in the lower bass staff. The top line gradually descends to the lower tones on the modal scale, thereby causing all the durations to be much longer. These differences in register and the extended durations help to increase the ominous mood of the depth of night. The last tones in the very low register extend over three measures, with brief interspersed rests and lead into the return of fear, a^2.

In the second couplet, section B' (measure 119), the repeated tone centered on low C begins with pianissimo intensity. Occasionally an upper neighbor, D-flat is added. The C tone is accented and increases in dynamics. The tritone occurs twice and the crescendo increases to f. Once more the long-eared owl enters b^2 in measure 125, giving the quick dissonant cry that is brief and ends abruptly. More weight is in the texture of the chords that make up this passage, which contains the same basic shape as before.

With unit c^2, little owl repeats the mewing, rapidly ascending passage of notes that places tones as well as rhythms counter to each other (measures 130 and 131).

Long-eared owl gives its call (b^3, measures 132 and 133) with an extension of the earlier passage. Now the cries grow softer, as staccato passages descend rapidly until they are nearly inaudible.

In unit c^3, measures 134 through 136, little owl interjects the "heartbeat-accelerating" yelps that usually complete his cry.

Tawny owl (d^2, measures 137 through 153) makes the final statement. Leaving out the sad and mournful cry, tawny owl repeats with added dissonance the intensely loud cry on C, which drops to the A natural. The other tones help create the timbre of this terror provoking bird by means of added resonance (see Example 51). The most important tone in the

Example 51. *Catalogue d'oiseaux,* "La chouette hulotte," section B', measures 137–138

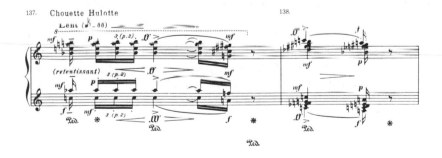

chord is marked with the greatest intensity, in double and triple forte (see brackets, Example 51). Now the call, with A rising to C, repeats the vague and terrifying sound, achieved with fifths in the right hand and clashing fourths in the left.

The strangely disquieting passage recurs, measures 144 through 146, now with longer extension of repetition, increasing the suspense. This time the unexpected silence is pierced with clamoring cries (measures 147 and 148) that Messiaen describes as "sounding like a child being murdered." The range of the chords in this passage is in the upper register at double forte intensity. The repeated chord (measure 148) is clashingly dissonant, with the main tones of the owl's call (beginning on C) standing out as the bottom line finally descends to A natural (see Example 52).

Now the C to A natural recurs in repeated chords (measures 149 through 151), with the second chord always in decreased intensity, as in the ending of a call. In these chords, containing augmented octaves and major sevenths, the two notes, C to A natural, pass to every position in the chord, lower to middle to upper tones (see Example 52).

A long silence intervenes. In the final measure, the chords of both hands consist entirely of the major seventh interval, now ascending a minor third to the next chord. Messiaen compares the passages of these tones to bells from another world.[4] The chords, decreasing in density of texture, have reversed their contour, now ascending a minor third to the next chord, with the C tone prominent in the first group and finally the A (last chord). This last chord sustains for a long resonating final effect.

"La chouette hulotte" illustrates Messiaen's use of musical notation to reproduce various birdcalls and their rhythmic patterns. He attempted in this work to convey time of day, habitat, and the passing of time. He also presents through the music the human emotions that the observer would experience in such a setting. Messiaen works with the twelve-tone pitch row that he uses freely, duplicating as nearly as possible the pitch of the birdsong. He provides added resonance by the use of dissonant intervals; and combines the use of monophonic, homophonic, and polyphonic textures. Chromatic rhythm is a characteristic feature of "La chouette hulotte"; his use of a mode of duration and intensities is an extension of the experimental period.

Example 52. *Catalogue d'oiseaux,* "La chouette hulotte," section *B'*, measures 146–153

*Marquer le *do* et le *la* du pouce de main droite.

Extract from *Catalogue d'oiseaux* by Olivier Messiaen. Copyright by Alphonse Leduc & Cie., Paris, France.

13

A Legacy

The 1960s began an era of recognition for Messiaen that has extended throughout the entire world. In addition to his built-in routine of composing, teaching, and playing the organ at la Trinité, Messiaen has managed to fit into his life a calendar of dates for world tours and lectures. He has been the subject of honor, receiving awards at festivals, universities, and premieres too numerous to cite in detail.

Messiaen and Yvonne Loriod, the interpreter of his piano works for many years, were married in 1962. They continue a busy professional life both in France and internationally. The Messiaens have resided in Paris during each school year, about three blocks from the metro system that easily takes him to la Trinité or to the Paris Conservatory.

In the summer Messiaen retreats to the countryside where he makes himself generally unavailable to demands from the outside world. This is his favorite time for composing and he tries to work without interruption on the ideas that have come to him during the year. Many summers he has chosen to spend in the Alps of the Dauphine, the locale of his childhood where he continues to collect the songs of birds.

Although his work as a composer is not yet finished, Messiaen has already provided a valuable legacy to the music of the twentieth century. He has written some exquisitely beautiful works that have earned him a growing audience worldwide. *Vingt regards sur l'Enfant Jésus* for piano is a three and one-half hour work that demands complete dedication on the part of the performing artist, as well as formidable technique. *Quatuor pour la fin du temps, Poèmes pour Mi,* and *Chants de terre et de ciel* appear regularly in the concert repertoire of leading chamber groups and soprano artists today. Messiaen's organ works are very popular with the leading soloists in the United States and Europe.

It has always been Messiaen's method of teaching to provide a very liberal atmosphere for discussion. His intention is to make his students aware of the very real problems of musical evolution and to this end he has always been truly engaged in the essential debate of today's music. Composer Jean Barraque, speaking of his studies with Messiaen, said:

One forgets that a truly great teacher brings nothing to his pupils, he rather provokes them. Although some expected Messiaen to establish a theory of analysis, he guarded himself against that. Only the works themselves matter, radiant and devastating. For him every work is a fresh mystery which he tackles with his own resources. Those with other resources are free to make different discoveries, other realizations.[1]

Among the works composed during the experimental years, "Mode de valeurs et d'intensitiés" became historically important because it realized the ultimate implications of serial music by placing duration in the proper perspective with the twelve-tone system. The *Quatre études* arrived at a structural synthesis using not only series of frequencies, but series of intensities, timbre, and duration. The revelation that has been considered the source of "totally" serial music was provided by Messiaen and became the point of departure for the avant-garde composers. With Messiaen's contribution, twentieth-century music had arrived at the beginning of a creative epoch wherein infinite possibilities existed.

Messiaen's pupils recognized this fact immediately. As early as 1948 Boulez wrote the Second Sonata for piano in which the tone-row concept expanded to include Messiaen's concepts of rhythmic organization as well as dynamics and articulation. Other works by Boulez which reflect this seed of Messiaen's discovery include *Polyphonie X* and *Le marteau sans maitre*. Stackhausen, fascinated by "Mode de valeurs et d'intensitiés," wrote Counterpoint No. 1 in 1953 and Piano Pieces Nos. 1–9 (1952–1954).

In the works following "Mode de valeurs" Messiaen has used the technique put forth there sparingly, and always in combination with the practices he has steadily developed throughout his creative lifetime. While some other modern composers may have become locked in by an exclusive use of serial techniques, Messiaen has avoided this danger. He has continued his interest in chromatic durations (see *Catalogue d'oiseaux*, chapt. 12) in *Chronochromie* (1960), using the technique of permutation as well as Greek rhythms. In *Chronochromie*, he used symmetrical permutation for the first time. This is a much less complex procedure than the infinite permutations that could result from the normal progression of thirty-two chromatic units. It is easily grasped if one realizes that only twelve durations could have 479,001,600 possible permutations. Messiaen has never been specific in explaining how he arrived at the order of thirty-six possible permutations.

In 1962 Messiaen composed *Sept haïkaï* for piano and small orchestra, which contains birdsong, permutations, and Greek meter in irrational values, all superimposed in independent layers. This work, *Chronochromie,* and *Couleurs de la cité céleste* (1963) are concerned with different aspects of color, which Messiaen has always related to sound.

The title of *Chronochromie* is derived from Greek words meaning "color of time." Messiaen is involved with rhythmic colorings in this work. *Sept haïkaï* contains chord patterns labeled by color in the score. In the third piece, *Couleurs de la cité céleste,* Messiaen arrives at the form by organizing colors that sound passages mean to him. In works of the early 1960s many harmonic colors are arrived at by serial means. During the latter half of the decade the use of modal color began to reappear.

Another major work written in the 1960s, *La transfiguration de notre Seigneur Jésus Christ,* contains many stylistic traits by now familiar to the reader: birdsong, modal colors, irrational rhythms, Hindu rhythms, Greek meters, and rhythmic permutations. It is Messiaen's first work for a very large choir and orchestra.

An innovation of the 1960s that occurred in the organ work *Méditations sur le mystère de la Sainte Trinité* (1969) is that of "communicable language." Messiaen introduced a mode of sounds, pitches, and durations that correspond to the alphabet so as to transform words into musical equivalents. The first performance of this work was March 20, 1972, in Washington, D.C. The musical and theological analysis that Messiaen wrote for the program of this performance are reproduced with his recording of the work. His alphabet stemmed from the attempt to transmit ideas, or speak, through music. Rather than provide a means of true language communication, this mode that uses the alphabet probably, and more important, provides the structure for the music.

Those who know him say that Messiaen's self-concept is indicative of an independent composer who belongs to no movements. He has remained aloof from influences of Viennese serialism; nor do the other major contemporary trends of electro-acoustics, aleatoricism, music theatre, or collage appear in his compositions. His work remains his own, so highly individualistic that it defies imitation. Perhaps that is why the style itself has not drawn followers from among his pupils. The creative mind does not usually find satisfaction in copying a style that belongs to another.

On the other hand, Messiaen may be considered a seminal composer because of the many innovations and revolutionary concepts that were taken up by his students and developed further in their own works. In addition to the concept of total organization that was introduced by Messiaen, it is likely that he has been responsible for the most significant development in rhythmic practice in the last three hundred years. After a long historical period of rhythmic regularity in Western music, Messiaen has redeveloped the principles of ancient metrics of a new level. By means of manipulation of the primary or minimum rhythmic value, he has created complexities of irrational and asymmetrical durations that would be impossible to conceive given the previous traditional rhythmic process. Messiaen's nonreversible rhythms (wherein a central unit is preceded and followed by symmetrical values) permit unity and diversity, another contribution used by today's composers. The technique of augmentation or diminution of a rhythmic part involves the altering of a metric balance by means of a note, a silence, or a dot.

Other rhythmic innovations of Messiaen's that were developed by his pupils involve the use of rhythmic cells, polyrhythms, and canonic forms. As a means of attaining structural coherence in Second Sonata, Boulez used his teacher's practice of rhythmic cell manipulation. This technique was also developed in the compositions Polyphonie X, String Quartet, and Polyphony for Eighteen Instruments. Boulez has also acknowledged his indebtedness to Messiaen for developing his interest in rhythmic canon, examples of which may be found in his Sonatina for flute and piano and Visage Nuptial.

Messiaen's presence in the twentieth century during one of music's evolutionary crises thus appears to be a necessary link and directional force. He has helped to unify such opposing voices as the defenders of so-called human music and the proponents of strict serialism. Just as he arrived at a creative synthesis of various elements in his own works, he represents the synthesis of opposing elements in contemporary music from which the next generation could proceed.

Messiaen is still composing music his own way. At present he is working on his first opera, having avoided the medium of theatre up to now. He discussed the future of music in his lecture at Brussels by saying,

Others will proceed in other ways. The electronic surrealists, the twelve-tone serialists may line up changes of register, isolated sounds and multi-form intensities; the stereophonists may displace sounding sources and create spatial counterpoints that are absolutely unheard in the proper sense of the word. There are a thousand ways of probing the future. I only wish that they would not forget that music is a part of time, . . . and that Nature, ever beautiful, ever great, ever new, Nature is the supreme resource.[2]

Notes and References

Chapter 1

1. Bernard Gavoty, "Who Are You, Olivier Messiaen?" *Tempo* 58 (Summer 1961):33–36.
2. Maurice Emmanuel, "Grèce," in *Encyclopédie de la musique et dictionnaire du composition* (Paris: Librairie Delagrave, 1924), 1:377–537.
3. *Conférence de Bruxelles prononcée a l'Exposition Internationale de Bruxelles en 1958* (Paris: Alphonse Leduc & Cie., 1960).
4. Table of 120 decî-tâla given in Albert Lavignac and Lionel de Laurencies, eds., *Encyclopédie de la musique et dictionnaire du composition* (Paris: Librairie Delagrave, 1924), 1:301–4.
5. *Technique de mon langage musical.* 2 vols. (Paris: Alphonse Leduc & Cie., 1944). English translation by John Satterfield, *The Technique of My Musical Language* (Paris: Alphonse Leduc & Cie., 1956).
6. *Technique* 1:33.
7. Ibid., 44. Term is used by Messiaen in the text.
8. As in "Antienne du silence" from *Chants de terre et de ciel.*
9. *Technique* 1:33.
10. Neumes are the notational signs used in the medieval manuscripts of Gregorian chant.
11. Benedictines of Solesmes, ed. *The liber usualis* (New York: Desclee & Cie., 1956).
12. Norman Demuth, "Messiaen and his organ music," *Musical Times* 96 (April 1955):203.
13. Gavoty, "Who are you, Olivier Messiaen?", 34.
14. Claude Samuel, *Entretiens avec Olivier Messiaen* (Paris: Editions Pierre Belfond, 1967).
15. Francis Routh, *Contemporary Music* (New York: Dover Publications, 1968), 68.
16. Curt Sachs, *Rhythm and Tempo* (New York: W. W. Norton & Co. 1953), 375–76.
17. For a discussion of isorhythm, see Donald Grout, *A History of Western Music.* (Revised edition; Boston: Allyn & Bacon, 1967).
18. *Technique* 1:24. This technique of rhythmic pedal, as defined by Messiaen, is the basic principle of isorhythm.
19. Willi Apel, "Isorhythmic," *Harvard Dictionary of Music.* 2nd ed. (Cambridge: Harvard University Press, 1969), 427.

20. Robert Sherlaw Johnson, *Messiaen* (London: Dent Publishers, 1975).

21. Paul Collaer, *A History of Modern Music* (New York: Grosset & Dunlap, 1961), 45–47. Generation implies, in this instance, the influence of the preceding musicians on subsequent groups of musicians.

22. Messiaen's modes are limited to a certain number of transpositions, as is the whole-tone scale. For this reason he calls them "modes of limited transposition."

23. Samuel, *Entretiens*, 125.

24. Routh, *Contemporary Music*, 37–40.

25. Gavoty, "Who Are You, Olivier Messiaen?" 36.

26. Antoine Golea, "French Music since 1945," *Musical Quarterly* 51 (January 1956):22.

27. Samuel, *Entretiens*, 66.

28. Jean Barraque, "Rhythme et developpement," *Polyphonie* 9 (1954):47–73.

29. Pierre Boulez, *Notes of an Apprenticeship* (New York: Alfred A. Knopf, 1968).

30. *Technique*, 1.

31. Ibid.

32. Johnson, *Messiaen*, 12.

33. *Technique*, 2:15.

34. Nicholas Slonimsky, *Music Since 1900* (New York: Coleman Ross Co., 1949), 411.

35. Claude Rostand, *French Music Today* (New York: Merlin Press, 1957), 41.

36. Johnson, *Messiaen*, 44.

37. Ibid., 113–14.

38. Trevor Hold, "Messiaen's Birds," *Music & Letters* 52 (April 1971):113–22.

Chapter 2

1. *Technique*

2. Ibid., 59.

3. Messiaen refers to the original mode as the first transposition; he also includes the original in counting the number of transpositions. Erroneous or not, this book remains consistent with the composer's terminology in this instance.

4. *Technique*, 58.

5. Ibid., 64.

6. In the production of electronic music, white sound, sometimes referred to as white noise, is that which contains all possible frequencies; it is not to be confused with the state of pantonality, a compositional approach.

7. *Technique*, 47.

8. Ibid., 50. In *Poèmes pour Mi*, chapter 6, Example 23, a whole series of the chord on the dominant illustrates the use of this technique.

9. Messiaen wrote *La nativité du Seigneur* and *Poèmes pour Mi* in first notation. Examples of this notation will also be found in chapters 5 and 6.

10. Notes to recording of Eight Preludes, Musical Heritage Society, MHS 1069.

11. Samuel, *Entretiens,* 125.

12. Pierrette Mari, *Olivier Messiaen: l'Homme et son Oeuvre* (Paris: Editions Seghers, 1965), 29.

Chapter 3

1. *Technique,* 1:65.
2. Ibid., 1:58.
3. Ibid., 1:64.
4. Ibid., 1:48; 2:34.
5. Ibid., 1:48.

Chapter 4

1. David Drew, "Messiaen—A Provisional Study," *Score,* 10 (December 1954), pp. 33–49.
2. Ibid., 63.
3. *Technique,* I:38.
4. Ibid., I:55.

Chapter 5

1. Notes to music of *La nativité du Seigneur* (Paris: Alphonse Leduc & Cie., 1936)
2. *The Bible* (Douay version), Zechariah, 9:9 (Messiaen's paraphrase).
3. *Technique,* Example 108.
4. Ibid., 1:31–32; 2:Examples 76 and 77.
5. Samuel, *Entretiens,* 42.
6. *Technique,* 1:56.

Chapter 6

1. Polymodality is different from polytonality, which is the superposition of two or more melodic fragments (or structures) written in different keys, rather than modes.
2. *Technique, I:69.*
3. Ibid., 1:17.
4. Ibid., 1:48.
5. Ibid., 1:50.

Chapter 7

1. Preface to score of *Quatuor pour la fin du temps* (Paris: Durand, 1941).
2. In this technique, two or more isorhythmic patterns appear simultaneously.
3. *Technique,* 2:11.
4. Ibid., 1:26.
5. Ibid., 1:51.
6. Preface to score of *Quatuor.*

Chapter 8

1. Preface to score of *Vingt regards sur l'Enfant Jésus* (Paris: Durand, 1944).
2. Ibid.
3. Rostand, *Olivier Messiaen* (Paris: Ventadour, 1968), 23.
4. For a table of augmentation and diminution, see *Technique*, 2:3.
5. *Technique*, I:19.
6. Ibid., 1:35.

Chapter 9

1. Notes to the recording of *Cinq rechants*, Philips Records (ABL-3400).
2. *Technique*, I:42.
3. Ibid. 1:15.
4. Ibid. 1:14.
5. For a discussion of the predominance of irregularity and variation of rhythmic formula in ancient Greece, see Emmanuel, "Grèce."
6. *Conférence de Bruxelles*, p. 3.

Chapter 10

1. Pierre Boulez, Jean Barraque, Yvonne Loriod, Karlheinz Stockhausen, et al., "Homage a Messiaen," *Melos* 25 (1958):386.
2. *Le livre d'orgue*, recorded at Sainte Trinité (Paris: Ducretet-Thomson, 1956).

Chapter 11

1. Drew, "Messiaen—A provisional study," p. 48.
2. *Technique*, 1:30.
3. Iwanka Krawtewa, "Le language rhythmique d'Olivier Messiaen et la metrique ancienne grecque," *Schweizerische Musikzeitung*, 112, (1972):82.
4. Samuel, *Entretiens*, p. 113.

Chapter 12

1. Samuel, *Entretiens, p. 95*.
2. Notes to the recording of *Catalogue d'oiseaux*, Erato, MHS 1423/4/5/6.
3. Samuel, *Entretiens*, p. 102.
4. Recording notes, *Catalogue d'oiseaux*.

Chapter 13

1. Pierre Boulez, Jean Barraque, Yvonne Loriod, Karlheinz Stockhausen, et al., "Homage a Messiaen," *Melos* 25 (1958):386.
2. *Conférence de Bruxelles*, p. 4.

Bibliography

Primary Sources

1. Books

Conférence de Bruxelles prononcée a l'Exposition Internationale de Bruxelles en 1958. Paris: Alphonse Leduc & Cie., 1960.
Technique de mon langage musical. 2 vols. Paris: Alphonse Leduc & Cie., 1944.
The Technique of My Musical Language. 2 vols. Translated by John Satterfield. Paris: Alphonse Leduc & Cie., 1956.
Vingt leçons d'harmonie. Paris: Alphonse Leduc & Cie., 1939.
Vingt leçons de solfege modernes. Paris: Henry Lemoine, 1934.

2. Music–Instrumental

Le merle noir pour flute et piano. Paris: Alphonse Leduc & Cie., 1952.
Quatuor pour la fin du temps. Paris: Durand & Cie., 1942.
Thème et variations pour violon et piano. Paris: Alphonse Leduc & Cie., 1934.

3. Music–Orchestral

L'ascension: Quatre meditations symphoniques pour orchestre. Paris: Alphonse Leduc & Cie., 1948.
Chronochromie pour grand orchestre. Paris: Alphonse Leduc & Cie., 1963.
Couleurs de la cité céleste pour piano, orchestre et percussions metalliques. Paris: Alphonse Leduc & Cie., 1966.
Et exspecto resurrectionem mortuorum pour orchestre de bois, cuivres, et percussions metalliques. Paris: Alphonse Leduc & Cie., 1966.
Les offrandes oubliées: Meditation symphonique pour orchestre. Paris: Durand & Cie., 1931.
Oiseaux exotiques pour piano solo et petit orchestre. London: Universal Edition, 1959.
Poèmes pour Mi pour grand soprano dramatique et orchestre. Paris: Durand & Cie., 1939.
Reveil des oiseaux pour piano solo et orchestre. Paris: Durand & Cie., 1955.
Sept haïkaï: esquisses Japonaises pour piano solo et petit orchestre. Paris: Alphonse Leduc & Cie, 1966.
Trois petites liturgies de la présence divine. Paris: Durand & Cie., 1952.
Turangalîla-symphonie pour piano principal et grand orchestre. Paris: Durand & Cie., 1953.

141

4. Music–Organ

Apparition de l'Église éternelle. Paris: Henry Lemoine, 1934.
L'ascension: Quatre meditations symphoniques pour orgue. Paris: Alphonse Leduc
     & Cie., 1934.
Le banquet céleste pour orgue. Paris: Alphonse Leduc & Cie., 1934.
Les corps glorieux: Sept visions breves de la vie des ressucites pour orgue. Paris:
     Alphonse Leduc & Cie., 1942.
Diptyque pour orgue. Paris: Durand & Cie., 1930.
Livre d'orgue: sept pieces pour orgue. Paris: Alphonse Leduc & Cie., 1953.
Meditations sur le mystère de la Sainte Trinité, Paris: Alphonse Leduc & Cie., 1973.
Messe de la Pentecôte pour orgue. Paris: Alphonse Leduc & Cie., 1951.
La nativité du Seigneur: neuf meditations pour orgue. Paris: Alphonse Leduc &
     Cie., 1936.
Verset pour la fête de la dédicace. Paris: Alphonse Leduc & Cie., 1961.

5. Music–Piano

Cantéyodjavâ pour piano. London: Universal Edition, 1953.
Catalogue d'oiseaux pour piano. Paris: Alphonse Leduc & Cie., 1964.
Fantaisie burlesque pour piano. Paris: Durand & Cie., 1932.
"Île de Feu 1" pour piano. Paris: Durand & Cie., 1950.
"Île de Feu 2" pour piano. Paris: Durand & Cie., 1950.
"Mode de valeurs et d'intensités" pour piano. Paris: Durand & Cie., 1950.
"Neumes rythmiques" pour piano. Paris: Durand & Cie., 1950.
Les offrandes oubliées, reduction pour piano. Paris: Durand & Cie., 1930.
Piece pour le tombeau de Paul Dukas. Paris: Revue Musicale de Mai-Juin, 1936.
Préludes pour pinao. Paris: Durand & Cie., 1930.
Rondeau pour piano. Paris: Durand & Cie., 1950.
Vingt regards sur l'Enfant Jésus pour piano. Paris: Durand & Cie., 1947.
Visions de l'Amen pour deux pianos. Durand & Cie., 1947.

6. Music–Vocal

Chants de terre et de ciel pour soprano et piano. Paris: Durand & Cie., 1939.
Cinq rechants pour douze voix mixtes. Paris: Editions Salabert, 1949.
Harawi: chant d'amour et de mort pour soprano et piano. Paris: Alphonse Leduc &
     Cie., 1948.
La mort du nombre pour soprano, tenor, violon et piano. Paris: Durand & Cie.,
     1931.
*O sacrum convivium! motet au Saint-Sacrement pour choeur a quatre voix mixtes ou
     quatre solistes.* Paris: Durand & Cie., 1937.
Poèmes pour Mi pour grand soprano dramatique et piano. Paris: Durand & Cie.,
     1937.
Trois melodies pour chant et piano. Paris: Durand & Cie., 1930.

Secondary Sources

1. Books

Benedictines of Solesmes, eds. *The liber usualis.* New York: Desclee & Cie., 1956. Complete volume of Gregorian chants. 668 pages.

Boulez, Pierre. *Notes of an apprenticeship.* New York: Alfred A. Knopf, 1968. Boulez discusses early musical growth and studies with Olivier Messiaen, as well as techniques of Messiaen. 398 pages.

Cope, David. *New directions in music.* Dubuque, Iowa: Wm. C. Brown Co., 1972. Relevant information on styles and techniques of new music covering the decades from 1950 to 1970. 140 pages.

Danielou, Alain. *Northern Indian music.* London: Christopher Johnson, 1949. A discussion of the concepts and philosophy of music of northern India. 235 pages.

Ewen, David. *Composers of tomorrow's music.* New York: Dodd, Mead & Co., 1971. Describes the current directions that various prominent composers are pursuing. The author discusses Messiaen's influence on many of the composers. 176 pages.

Fox-Strangways, A. H. *The music of Hindustan.* London: Oxford at the Clarendon Press, 1914. Discusses the philosophy and practices of Hindustan music. 348 pages.

Goldron, Romain. *Ancient and Oriental music.* New York: Doubleday & Co., 1968. An introductory study. 127 pages.

Golea, Antoine. *Contemporary music in Europe: a comprehensive survey.* Edited by Lang & Broder. New York: G. Schirmer, 1965. Historical survey of European contemporary music is comprehensive and includes critical insight. 308 pages.

Grout, Donald J. *A history of Western music.* Rev. ed. Boston: Allyn & Bacon, 1967. Well-known volume of music history provides concise information concerning all facets of Western musical styles and periods. 742 pages.

Hodeir, Andre. *Since Debussy: a view of contemporary music.* New York: Grove Press, 1961. Critical and analytical discussion of the contemporary music that followed Debussy. Hodier sharply criticizes some of the innovative practices Messiaen has introduced. 256 pages.

Johnson, Robert Sherlaw. *Messiaen.* London: Dent Publishers, 1975. This survey of all of Messiaen's music discusses various techniques of the composer, illustrating them with music examples. 221 pages.

Mari, Pierrette. *Olivier Messiaen: l'homme et son oeuvre.* Paris: Editions Seghers, 1965. This small volume, in French, contains a biographical section and a brief discussion of Messiaen's works. 191 pages.

Nichols, Roger. *Messiaen.* New York: Oxford University Press, 1975. Short introductory study discusses various aspects of Messiaen's music and creative evolution. 79 pages.

Rostand, Claude. *Twentieth century music.* Edited by Rollo Myers. New York: Orion Press, 1970. General historical and critical study concerning music of the twentieth century. 189 pages.

Rostand, Claude. *Olivier Messiaen.* Paris: Ventadour, 1957. Interesting volume provides insight into the composer and his craft. 178 pages.

Routh, Francis. *Contemporary music: an introduction.* New York: Dover Publications, 1968. Introductory study of contemporary music and major composers. 191 pages.

Sachs, Curt. *Rhythm and tempo.* New York: W. W. Norton & Co., 1953. Discussion of rhythmic practices from ancient times to the present midcentury. 391 pages.

Samuel, Claude. *Entretiens avec Olivier Messiaen.* Paris: Editions Pierre Belfond, 1967. Presents seven interviews Samuel had with Messiaen concerning a variety of topics related to his compositions. 140 pages.

Waumsley, Stuart. *The organ music of Olivier Messiaen.* Paris: Alphonse Leduc & Cie., 1968. Concentrates on the organ music of Messiaen and presents theoretical information. 56 pages.

2. Articles

Barraque, Jean. "Rythme et developpement," *Polyphonie* 9 (1954):47–73. Analytical study of rhythm and an account of Messiaen's illuminating analysis of *Le Sacre du printemps* by Stravinsky.

Bell, Carla Huston. "Olivier Messiaen," *Music Journal* 39 (September 1978):8–10. Discusses the evolution of Messiaen's sixty years as a composer and his influence on music of the future.

Birkby, Arthur. "Interview with France's noted organist and composer," *Clavier* 11:3 (March 1972):18–20. Messiaen discusses tempo and timbre with *Clavier's* organ editor.

Boulez, Pierre; Barraque, Jean; Loriod, Yvonne; Stockhausen, Karlheinz; et al. "Homage a Messiaen," *Melos* 25 (1958):386. In honor of Messiaen's fiftieth birthday, several composers pay tribute to him by discussing the memorable and fascinating aspects of his personality and teaching.

Dickinson, Peter. "Messiaen—composer of crisis," *Music and Musicians* 10 (October 1966):26–30. Discusses Messiaen's music in relation to the spiritual crisis of the age.

Drew, David. "Messiaen—a provisional study," *Score,* part 1, no. 10 (December 1954):33–49; part 2, no. 13 (September 1955):59–73; part 3, no. 14 (December 1955):41–61. Early comprehensive study of the composer's music divided into three articles.

Gardiner, Bennitt. "Dialogues with Messiaen," *Musical Events* (October 1967):6–9. Summary of the conversations Messiaen had with French musicologist, Claude Samuel.

———. "Great French musician, Olivier Messiaen," *Musical Events* 22 (April 1967):12–14. Biographical sketch and assessment of the composer's work.

Gavoty, Bernard. "Who are you, Olivier Messiaen?" *Tempo* 58 (Summer 1961):33–36. Interview with the composer provides insight into his esthetic.

Golea, Antoine. "French music since 1945," *Musical Quarterly* 51:1 (January 1965):22–37. In this discussion of the music of France during the past twenty-five years, Golea mentions that Messiaen is the only professor at Paris Conservatory who provides inspiration to the new composers.

Hold, Trevor. "Messiaen's birds," *Music and Letters* 52:2 (April 1971):112–22. Detailed discussion about the technique of birdsong in Messiaen's music assesses the question of whether they are authentic transcriptions of the birds' songs.

Krastewa, Iwanks. "Le langage rhythmique d'Olivier Messiaen et la metrique ancienne Grecque," *Schweizerische Musikzeitung* 112 (January-February 1972):79–86. Discusses the Greek *chronos protos* and its influence on Messiaen's concept of rhythm.

Lyons, David Spence. "Olivier Messiaen," *Music in Education* 31:327 (1967):567–70. Discussion of Messiaen's place in the contemporary musical scene.

Quenetain, Tanneguy de. "Messiaen, poet of nature," *Realites* 45 (December 1962); see also *Music and Musicians* 2:9 (May 1963):8–12. The role of nature's influence on Messiaen's craft and way of life.

Samuel, Claude. "Olivier Messiaen," *Music and Musicians* 21 (April 1973):44–47. Brief essay on the composer and his place in major contemporary trends.

Smalley, Roger. "Debussy and Messiaen," *Musical Times* 109:1499 (February 1968):128–31 Study of the influence of Debussy on Messiaen's music cites similarities and differences.

Wen-Chung, Chou. "Asian concepts and tenth century Western composers," *Musical Quarterly* 57:1 (1971):211–29. Asian concepts and their influence on some twentieth-century composers, including Messiaen.

3. Dictionaries and Encyclopedias

Apel, Willi. *Harvard Dictionary of Music*. 2nd rev. ed. Cambridge: Harvard University Press, 1969.

Bake, Arnold. "Music of India." In *New Oxford dictionary*. Oxford: Oxford University Press, 1969.

Blom, Eric, ed. *Grove's dictionary of music and musicians*. 5th ed. London: Macmillan Publishing Co., 1954.

Emmanuel, Maurice. "Grèce." In *Encyclopédie de la musique et dictionnaire du composition*. Vol. I. Paris: Librairie Delagrave, 1924, 377.

Grosset, M. J. "Inde." In *Encyclopédie de la musique et dictionnaire du composition*. Vol. I. Paris: Librairie Delagrave, 1924, 296–304.

Lavignac, Albert, and de Laurencies, Lionel, eds. *Encyclopédie de la musique et dictionnaire du composition*. Vol. I (Antiquite-Moyen Age). Paris: Librairie Delagrave, 1924. Contains sections on Greek and Indian music, including one hundred twenty decî-tâlas according to Çârngadeva.

4. Dissertations

Adams, Beverly Decker. *The organ compositions of Olivier Messiaen.* Ph.D. dissertation, University of Utah, 1969. Available from Xerox University Microfilms, Ann Arbor, Michigan. This study analyzes all the organ compositions of Olivier Messiaen from formal and technical viewpoints.

Bell, Carla Huston. *A structural and stylistic analysis of representative works by Olivier Messiaen,* D. Ed. dissertation, Columbia University, 1977. Compositions from various performance mediums are examined; the study covers the comprehensive periods of Messiaen's creative life. The analysis examines compositional techniques in the areas of form, harmony, timbre, melody, and rhythm.

List of Works

1917 *Le Dame de Shalott* for piano.

1921 *Deux ballades de Villon* for voice and piano.

1925 *La tristesse d'un grand ciel blanc* for piano.

1926 *Le banquet céleste* for organ (Paris: Alphonse Leduc, 1934, 1960).

1927 *Esquisse modale* for organ.

     L'hote aimable des ames for organ.

     Le banquet Eucharistique for orchestra.

     Variations ecossaises for organ.

1929 *Préludes* for piano (Paris: Durand, 1930).

1930 *Diptyque* for organ (Paris: Durand, 1930).

     La mort du nombre for soprano, tenor, violin, and piano.

     Les offrandes oubliées for orchestra (Paris: Durand, 1931).

     Les offrandes oubliées for piano reduction (Paris: Durand, 1931).

     Simple chant d'une ame for orchestra.

     Trois melodies for soprano and piano (Paris: Durand, 1930).

1931 *Le tombeau resplendissant* for orchestra (Paris: Durand, rental).

1932 *Apparition de l'eglise éternelle* for organ (Paris: Lemoine, 1934).

     Fantaisie burlesque for piano (Paris: Durand, 1932).

     Hymne au Saint-Sacrement for orchestra (Paris: Broude, 1970).

     Thème et variations for violin and piano (Paris: Alphonse Leduc, 1934).

1933 *Fantaisie* for violin and piano.

     L'ascension for orchestra (Paris: Alphonse Leduc, 1934).

     Messe for eight sopranos and four violins.

1935 *La nativité du Seigneur* for organ (Paris: Alphonse Leduc, 1936).

     Piece pour le tombeau de Dukas for piano (Paris: *Revue Musicale*, Mai-Juin 1936).

Vocalise for soprano and piano (Paris: Durand, 1937).

1936   *Poèmes pour Mi* for soprano and piano (Paris: Durand, 1937).

1937   *Fête des belles eaux* for Ondes Martenot.

      O sacrum convivium! for choir (Paris: Durand, 1937).

      Poèmes pour Mi for soprano and orchestra (Paris: Durand, 1939).

1938   *Chants de terre et de ciel* for soprano and piano (Paris: Durand, 1939).

      Deux monodies for Ondes Martenot.

1939   *Les corps glorieux* for organ (Paris: Alphonse Leduc, 1942).

      Vingt leçons d'harmonie (Paris: Alphonse Leduc, 1939).

1941   *Choeurs pour une Jeanne d'Arc* for large and small mixed choirs. *Quatuor pour la fin du temps* for chamber orchestra (Paris: Durand, 1942).

1942   *Musique de scene pour un Oedipe* for Ondes Martenot.

1943   *Rondeau* for piano (Paris: Alphonse Leduc, 1943).

      Visions de l'Amen for two pianos (Paris: Durand, 1950).

1944   *Trois petites liturgies de la présence divine* for choir, Ondes Martenot, and orchestra (Paris: Durand, 1952).

      Technique de mon langage musical (Paris: Alphonse Leduc, 1944).

1944   *Vingt regards sur l'Enfant Jésus* for piano (Paris: Durand, 1947).

1945   *Harawi, chant d'amour et de mort* for soprano and piano (Paris: Alphonse Leduc, 1948).

1946–1948   *Turangalîla-symphonie* for piano, Ondes Martenot, and orchestra (Paris: Durand, 1953).

1949   *Cantéyodjayâ* for piano (London: Universal Edition, 1953).

1949   *Cinq rechants* for mixed choir (Paris: Editions Salabert, 1949).

1949–1950   *Quatre études de rhythme* for piano (Paris: Durand, 1950).

1950   *Quatre études de rythme* for piano (Paris: Durand, 1950).

1950   *Messe de la Pentecôte* for organ (Paris: Alphonse Leduc, 1951).

1951   *Le livre d'orgue* for organ (Paris: Alphonse Leduc, 1953).

1952   *Le merle noir* for flute and piano (Paris: Alphonse Leduc, 1952). *Timbres durées* for musique concrete.

1953   *Reveil des oiseaux* for piano and orchestra (Paris: Durand, 1959). *Soixante-quatre leçons d'harmonie* (Paris: Alphonse Leduc, 1953).

1956 *Oiseaux exotiques* for piano and small orchestra. (London: Universal Edition, 1959).

1956–1958 *Catalogue d'oiseaux* for piano (Paris: Alphonse Leduc, 1963).

1960 *Chronochromie* for orchestra (Paris: Alphonse Leduc, 1963).
Verset pour la fête de la dédicace for organ (Paris: Alphonse Leduc, 1963).

1962 *Sept haïkaï* for small orchestra (Paris: Alphonse Leduc, 1966).

1963 *Couleurs de la cité céleste* for small orchestra (Paris: Alphonse Leduc, 1966).

1964 *Et exspecto resurrectionem mortuorum* for winds, strings, and metallic percussion (Paris: Alphonse Leduc, 1966).

1963–1969 *La transfiguration de notre Seigneur Jésus-Christ* for orchestra and choir (Paris: Alphonse Leduc, 1972).

1969 *Meditations sur le mystère de la Sainte Trinité* for organ (Paris: Alphonse Leduc, 1973).

Discography

Because of the international stature of the composer, Olivier Messiaen, this discography includes important recordings that have been made in the United States, Great Britain, France, and Germany. Listings are confined to the most prominent artists and conductors in these countries, as well as to the most easily obtainable record labels within the countries mentioned.

Apparition de l'Église éternelle. Charles Krigbaum. Work includes *l'ascension* and *Banquet.* Lyrichord 7297.

L'ascension. Charles Krigbaum. Work includes *Apparition* and *Banquet.* Lyrichord 7297.

L'ascension. Simon Preston at Chapel of King's College, Cambridge. Work includes Franck: Choral No. 2, *Piece Heroique.* Argo ZRG 5339.

L'ascension. Olivier Messiaen at the organ of la Trinité, Paris. Ducretet-Thomson, DUC 1.

L'ascension. No. 3. Jean-Claude Reynaud. Decca/Turnabout 34319 S.

L'ascension. Nos. 3 and 4. Christopher Herrick. Gamut/Vista 1001.

L'ascension. Stokowski conducting the New York Philharmonic Orchestra (first recording). Columbia ML 4214.

L'ascension. Stokowski conducting the London Philharmonic Orchestra (second recording). London SPC 21060.

L'ascension. Marius Constant conducting Orchestre Philharmonique de l'ORTF. Work includes *Les offrandes oubliées, Hymne au Saint Sacrement.* Erato STU 70673.

Le banquet céleste. Charles Krigbaum. Work includes *Apparition, L'ascension.* Lyrichord 7297.

Le banquet céleste. Marcel Dupré. Work includes *Les bergers.* Mercury 75088.

Le banquet céleste. Stephen Cleobury. Grosvenor 1006.

Cantéyodjavâ. Yvonne Loriod, piano; Pierre Boulez, conductor. Work includes Boulez, *Sonatine pour flute et piano;* Stockhausen, *Zeitmasse,* and Berio, *Serenata 1.* Vega C 30 A 139.

Cantéyodjavâ. Robert Sherlaw Johnson. Work includes "Neumes rythmiques," "Ile de Feu I and II." Argo ZRG 694.

Catalogue d'oiseaux. Jocy de Oliveira. SVBX 5464.

Catalogue d'oiseaux. Yvonne Loriod. Vega UAL 11 (3 discs); Erato-STU 70595-98 (4 discs).

Catalogue d'oiseaux, Nos. 2, 5, 6, 9, 12. Yvonne Loriod. Work includes *Cantéyod-jayâ*, *Turangalîla-symphonie*, and *Visions de l'Amen*. Int. Pilgrims Group 279031/34.

Catalogue d'oiseaux No. 9. Yvonne Loriod. Work includes *Oiseaux exotiques*, *Reveil des oiseaux*. Eurodisc 913.128.

Chants de terre et de ciel. Noelle Barker, soprano; Robert Sherlaw Johnson, piano. Work includes *Poèmes pour Mi*. Argo ZRG 699.

Chronochromie. Antal Dorati conducting the BBC Symphony Orchestra. Work includes Boulez, *Le soleil des eaux;* and Koechlin, *Les barndar-log*, Op. 176. ZRG 758.

Cinq rechants. New England Conservatory Chorus. Golden Crest NEC 117.

Cinq rechants. John Alldis conducting John Alldis Choir. Work includes Bruckner, Four Sacred Motets; Schoenberg, *Friede auf erden;* and Debussy, Three Part Songs. Argo ZRG 523.

Cinq rechants. Marcel Courand conducting Les Solistes des Choeurs de l'ORTF. Work includes Xenakis, *Nuits;* and Penderecki, *Stabat mater*. Erato STU 70457.

Les corps glorieux. Charles Krigbaum. Lyrichord 7224.

Les corps glorieux. Louis Thiry. Work includes *Apparition, l'ascension, Messe*, and *Verset*. Calliope 1.925/27.

Les corps glorieux. Simon Preston in the Cathedral and Abbey Church of St. Albans. Work includes *Le banquet céleste*. Argo ZRG 633.

Les corps glorieux, Nos. 2, 3. Jean-Claude Reynaud. Decca/Vox 657.

Les corps glorieux. Olivier Messiaen at the organ of la Trinité, Paris. Work includes *Apparition de l'Église éternelle*. Ducretet Thomson, DUC 4 & 5.

Les corps glorieux. Almut Rossler at the Rieger organ of Neanderkuche, Dusseldorf, West Germany. Schwann ams Studio 509.

Couleurs de la cité céleste. Pierre Boulez, conducting the orchestre du Domaine Musical; Strassbourg Percussion Ensemble; Yvonne Loriod, piano. Work includes *Et exspecto resurrectionem mortuorum*. CBS 3 21 10048; Columbia MS 7356; Erato STU 70302.

Des canyons aux etoiles. Yvonne Loriod. Marius Constant directing Ensemble Ars Nova. Erato STU 70.974/75.

Diptyque. Louis Thiry. Work includes *Banquet; Livre d'orgue;* and *Nativité*. Calliope 1.928/30.

Et exspecto resurrectionem mortuorum. Serge Baude conducting the Orchestre de Paris. Work includes *Les offrandes oubliées*. Angel S-36559; Voix de son Maitre CBS 2121.

Et exspecto resurrectionem mortuorum. Pierre Boulez conducting Orchestre du Domaine Musical; Strassbourg Percussion Ensemble; Yvonne Loriod, piano. Work includes *Couleurs de la cité céleste*. CBS 3 21 10048; Columbia MS 7356; Erato STU 70302.

Fête des belles eaux pour sextour d'Ondes Martenot. Jeanne Loriod, Nelly Caron, Monique Matagne, Renee Recoussine, Karel Trou, Henriette Chanforan. Work includes Milhaud, Suite; and Charpentier, *Lolita.* Erato STU 70102.

Harawi. Noelle Barker, soprano; Robert Sherlaw Johnson, piano. Argo ZRG 605.

Hymne au Saint-Sacrement. Marius Constant conducting the Orchestre Philharmonique de l'ORTF. Work includes *L'ascension,* and *Les offrandes oubliées.* Erato STU 70673.

Livre d'orgue. Louis Thiry. Work includes *Banquet, Diptyque,* and *Nativité.* Calliope 1.928/30.

Livre d'orgue. Almut Rossler at the Rieger organ of Neanderkirche, Dusseldorf, West Germany. Schwann ams Studio 506.

Meditations sur le mystère de la Sainte Trinité. Olivier Messiaen at the organ of la Trinité, Paris. Erato STU 70.750/51.

Meditations sur le mystère de la Sainte Trinité. Almut Rossler at the Becherath organ of Johanneskirche, Dusseldorf, West Germany. Schwann ams Studio 702/703.

Melodies pour soprano et piano. Michelle Command, soprano; Marie-Madeleine Petit, piano. Work includes *Chants de terre et de ciel, Harawi,* and *Poèmes pour Mi.* Voix de son Maitre C 167-16.226/28.

Le merle noir. Wolfgang Schulz, flute; Helmut Deutsch. Telefunken 6.42364.

Le merle noir. Paige Brooke, flute; Robert Levin, piano; Decca/Vox 670; Candide 31050.

Le merle noir. James Pellerite, flute; Charles Webb, piano. Coronet S 1713.

Le merle noir. Severino Gazzelloni, flute; Aloys Kontarsky, piano. Time 58008.

Messe de la Pentecôte. Olivier Messiaen at the organ of la Trinité. Ducretet-Thomson DUC 6.

Messe de la Pentecôte. Charles Krigbaum. Lyrichord 7226.

Messe de la Pentecôte. Louis Thiry. Work includes *Apparition, L'ascension, Corps glorieux,* and *Verset.* Calliope 1.925/27.

Messe de la Pentecôte, Nos. 4 & 5. Jean-Claude Reynaud. Decca/Vox 657.

Messe de la Pentecôte; Verset pour la fête de la dédicace. Almut Rossler at the Rieger organ of Neanderkirche, Dusseldorf, West Germany. Schwans ams Studio 508.

La nativité du Seigneur. Olivier Messiaen at the organ of la Trinité. Work includes *Diptyque.* Ducretet-Thomson. DUC 2 and 3.

La nativité du Seigneur. Charles Krigbaum. Lyrichord 7225.

La nativité du Seigneur. Simon Preston at Westminster Abbey. Argo ZRG 5447.

La nativité du Seigneur. Louis Thiry. Work includes *Banquet, Diptyque,* and *Livre d'orgue.* Calliope 1.928/30.

La nativité du Seigneur. Jean-Claude Reynaud. Decca/Vox 657.

La nativité du Seigneur. Gillian Weir at Royal Festival Hall, London. Radner Recordings SRR 2503 & 2504.

154 OLIVIER MESSIAEN

La nativité du Seigneur. Ernest White at Methuen Memorial Hall, Methuen, Massachusetts. Mercury MC 10069.

O sacrum convivium! St. John's College Chorus, Cambridge; Guest (organ). Work includes Faure, *Durufle, Messe;* and Poulenc, *Langlais, Litanies.* Argo ZRG 662.

O sacrum convivium! Worcester Cathedral Choir. Cassion/Abbey 680.

O sacrum convivium! Choirs of York Minster, Chapel Royal, St. James's Palace. Cassion/Abbey 717.

Les offrandes oubliées. Marious Constant conducting the Orchestre Philharmonique de l'ORTF. Work includes *L'ascension,* and *Hymne au Saint Sacrement.* Erato STU 70673.

Les offrandes oubliées. Serge Baudo conducting the Orchestre de Paris. Work includes *Et exspecto resurrectionem mortuorum.* Voix de son Maitre CVB 2121; Angel S 36559.

Oiseaux exotiques. Yvonne Loriod, piano. Vaclar Neumann conducting the Czech Philharmonic Orchestra. Work includes *Catalogue d'oiseaux,* No. 9, and *Reveil des oiseaux.* Candide CE 31002; Eurodisc 913.128. Pinnacle/Supraphon 748/749.

Oiseaux exotiques. Yvonne Loriod, piano. Rudolfe Albert conducting Orchestre Concert Domaine Musical. Includes works of Gabrieli, Henze, and Stravinsky. Vega C 30 A 65.

Poèmes pour Mi. Noelle Barker, soprano; Robert Sherlaw Johnson, piano. Work includes *Chants de terre et de ciel.* Argo ZRG 699.

Poèmes pour Mi. Lise Arseguet, soprano; Olivier Messiaen, piano. Everest 3269.

Préludes pour piano. Yvonne Loriod. Work includes *Quatre études de rythme.* Erato STU 70433.

Quatuor pour la fin du temps. Jean Pasquier, violin; Olivier Messiaen, piano; Andre Vacellier, clarinet; Etienne Pasquier, cello. Musidisc 34429.

Quatuor pour la fin du temps. Huguette Fernandez, violin; Marie-Madeline Petit, piano; Guy Deplus, clarinette; Jacques Neilz, clarinet. Erato STU 60156.

Quatuor pour la fin du temps. Luben Yordanoff, violin; Claude Desurmont, clarinet; Albert Tetard, cello; Daniel Barenboim, piano. Deutsche Grammophon 2531093.

Quatuor pour la fin du temps. Gervase De Peyer, clarinet; Michel Beroff, piano; Erich Gruenberg, violin; William Pleeth, cello. Voix de son Maitre C 06301.858.

Quatuor pour la fin du temps. Ida Kavafian, violin; R. Stoltzman, clarinet; Fred Sherry, cello; Peter Serkin, piano. RCA RL 11.567.

Quatre études de rythme. Yvonne Loriod, piano. Work includes *Préludes.* Erato STU 70433.

Quatre études de rythme. Olivier Messiaen, piano. (78 RPM) Columbia LFX 998-999.

Reveil des oiseaux. Yvonne Loriod, piano; Vaclav Neumann conducting the Czech

Philharmonic Orchestra. Work includes *Catalogue d'oiseaux,* No. 9, and *Oiseaux exotiques.* Candid CE 31002; Erato STU 70409.

Sept haïkaï. Yvonne Loriod, piano; Pierre Boulez conducting the Domaine Musical Orchestra; Strassbourg Percussion Ensemble. Work includes Schoenberg, Chamber Symphony, Op. 9, and Three Pieces for Orchestra. Everest 3192; Ades 15004.

Sept haïkaï. Yvonne Loriod, piano. Marius Constant conducting the Ensemble Ars Nova. Erato STU 70.796.

Thème et variations. G. Banat. Turnabout 34429.

La transfiguration de notre Seigneur Jésus-Christ. Westminster Choir College Choir; Antal Dorati conducting the National Symphony Orchestra. Decca/ Head 1-2.

Trois petite liturgies de la présence divine. Marcel Courand conducting Chamber Orchestra of l'ORTF. Yvonne Loriod, piano; Jeanne Loriod, Ondes Martenot. Erato STU 70200.

Trois petite liturgies de la Présence divine. Marcel Courand conducting vocal ensemble; Andre Giraud conducting chamber orchestra; Yvonne Loriod, piano; Jeanne Loriod, Ondes Martenot. Ducretet-Thomson 270 C 075.

Trois petite liturgies de la présence divine. Leonard Bernstein conducting Choral Art Society; New York Philharmonic Orchestra; Paul Jacobs, piano; John Canarina, Ondes Martenot. Work includes Roussel, Symphony No. 3 in G Minor. Columbia MS 6582.

Turangalîla-symphonie. Jeanne and Yvonne Loriod, pianos; Seiji Ozawa conducting Toronto Symphony Orchestra. Work includes Roussel, Symphony No. 3 in G Minor. Columbia MS 6582.

Turangalîla-symphonie. Yvonne and Jeanne Loriod, painos; Maurice Le Roux conducting National Orchestra RTF. Decca 117013/14; International Pilgrims Group 279.031/34.

Turangalîla-symphonie. Andre Previn conducting the London Symphony; Yvonne Loriod and Michael Beroff, pianos. Voix de son Maitre/EMI C 167 02.974/75.

Verset pour la fête de la dédicace. Louis Thiry. Work includes *Apparition, L'ascension, Corps glorieux,* and *Messe.* Calliope 1.925/27.

Vingt regards sur l'Enfant Jésus. Michael Beroff, piano. Voix de son Maitre C 181 11.117/18. (3 records).

Vingt regards sur l'Enfant Jésus. Yvonne Loriod, piano. Vega 8500-02 (3 records).

Vingt regards sur l'Enfant Jésus. John Ogden, piano. Argo ZRG 650/51.

Vingt regards sur l'Enfant Jésus. Peter Serkin, piano. RCA-CRL 3-0759.

Vingt regards sur l'Enfant Jésus. Jocy de Oliveira, piano. SVBX 5486.

Visions de l'Amen. Katia and Marielle Labeque. Erato STU 70567.

Visions de l'Amen. Yvonne Loriod and Olivier Messiaen, pianos. Vega 8509.

Visions de l'Amen. John Ogdon and Brenda Lucas, pianos. Argo ZRG 665.

Visions de l'Amen. Peter Serkin and Yuji Takahashi, pianos. RCA ARL 1-0363.

Index